ADDITIONAL PRAISE FOR ACCOUNTING DISRUPTED: HOW DIGITALIZATION IS CHANGING FINANCE

"Accounting Disrupted is a gamechanger. It will recharge accounting in readiness for the next decade. Ignore this book at your peril."

—Teemu Malmi, Professor, Aalto University

"At a time when the digital economy is disrupting business models and reshaping P&Ls, Al shows us its impact on accounting. He reveals how business leaders can tackle this critical transformation proactively and thoughtfully."

—Salman Amin, Chief Executive Officer, Pladis Foods Ltd.

"Anyone interested in the way digital technologies are transforming accounting, and accounting's role in the financial management of an organization resulting from this digital transformation, needs to read this book!

—Lawrence Gordon, Professor, Smith School of Business, University of Maryland

"Digital technologies are reshaping business, accounting, and financial services. *Accounting Disrupted* shows how finance can buttress digital transformations with sharp insight and experience-based focus. No finance leader can afford to ignore this book."

—Ashok Vadgama, President, CAM-I

"Every CFO today faces the challenge of navigating their business and finance function through a digital transformation. Al Bhimani's book show us how to unlearn our analog mindset and reboot it for digital leadership."

—Jussi Siitonen, Chief Financial Officer, Amer Sports

"Bhimani's book is a masterful blend of insight and professional relevance on digitalization – the greatest challenge facing accounting and finance today."

—Salvador Carmona, Professor, Rector, IE University

Accounting Disrupted

Accounting Disrupted

How Digitalization Is Changing Finance

Al Bhimani

WILEY

Published by John Wiley & Sons, Inc., Hoboken, New Jersey.
Published simultaneously in Canada.

For general information on our other products and services or for technical support,
please contact our Customer Care Department within the United States at (800) 762-
2974, outside the United States at (317) 572-3993, or fax (317) 572-4002.

Wiley publishes in a variety of print and electronic formats and by print-on-demand.
Some material included with standard print versions of this book may not be included
in e-books or in print-on-demand. If this book refers to media such as a CD or DVD
that is not included in the version you purchased, you may download this material at
http://booksupport.wiley.com. For more information about Wiley products, visit www
.wiley.com.

Library of Congress Cataloging-in-Publication Data is Available:

ISBN 9781119720065 (hardcover)
ISBN 9781119720119 (ePDF)
ISBN 9781119720096 (ePub)

Cover Design: Wiley
Cover Image: © slavemotion/Getty Images

SKY10024248_012121

For Farah

Contents

Preface

Digitalization is the biggest transformation in the history of business, and the scale of disruption is palpable within every organization. Digital technologies are being applied across many enterprises at supercharged speed, creating new business models just as traditional ones are being destroyed. What is most striking is the incompatibility of conventional managerial knowledge and operating tools with the challenges and opportunities digital brings. *Adeptness* and *agility* are the catchwords in the new economic future being created, but little can happen in the absence of informed insight. This book is about how financial intelligence must become current with the effects and potential of digital transformations in business. Until now, accounting and financial reporting has been a key driver of decisions across every imaginable organizational context. In a world where managing is reliant on knowing about economic transactions, accounting information is invaluable. That world, however, is ceasing to exist as fast as forms of data are diversifying, and their sources multiplying. No executive can continue to depend on the narrow representation provided by traditional financial reports.

Predictive data drawn from a vast network of sources are not just essential for survival but can supercharge enterprise growth. Digital technologies are about just that – the reshaping of exchanges, and the production and analysis of data to direct executive action. Moreover, automated machines are developing the capacity to make more and more decisions. This represents a shift from human-based work to machine-determined action. Further still, products can themselves emit data that will eliminate the need for remote information systems, including conventional accounting controls. These changes take accounting's potential into a new realm. Finance professionals must loop into this.

This book starts by discussing broad forces of change that affect accounting. It explains major digital technologies that are transforming organizations and impacting finance work and explores the following in relation to how accounting is being disrupted by digital:

- How do data analytics, robots, AI technologies, and blockchains enhance accounting?
- Why are finance leaders carriers of the greatest expertise risk?
- What are new roles in advisory, security, governance, and regulation for finance people?
- How close are we to total population audits and continuous reporting?
- Will blockchain systems disintermediate auditors?
- Why are strategic and operational activities intertwined as digitalization advances?
- Why is size crucial in attaining digital threshold points?
- Why do expenses drive revenues in digitalized firms?
- How can costs be managed other than through volume and scope changes in digital?
- Is activity-based costing still useful?
- Should workers set their own performance evaluation targets?
- Why are dividing lines between operating expenses and capital expenditures crumbling?
- Does soft information still matter in highly data-centric firms?
- Does automation affect the quality of audit evidence and output?
- Is learning from data becoming the new organizational power tool?
- How should finance teams partner with data scientists?
- Is there a right mix of technical versus social skills in digital?
- What new risks must the finance function tackle?
- How can the right level of cybersecurity investment be determined?
- What are the hidden sides of data?

These and other questions are answered in the book, drawing on the experiences of global enterprises that are digitalizing, including: IBM, Banco Santander, Airbnb, Wipro, Skyscanner, Unilever, Nestle, Maersk, Barclays, Accenture, Fidelity, Ping An Bank, Walmart, and the Big Four firms, among others.

The book will prove invaluable to finance professionals, CFOs, auditors, management and public accountants, accountancy students, as well as business and accounting educators. It is also essential reading for business managers who wish to know what to expect from the finance function. No one with an interest in finance work can afford to ignore the changes created by digitalization. Accounting is in a deep state of disruption – one that brings more possibilities for moving forward than any other transformational force the field has witnessed. Staying in place is not an option. What accounting and finance leaders must now understand about digital is captured in the pages that follow.

Acknowledgments

Many people have helped write this book. I must first thank Barry Melancon, who leads AICPA, for immediately seeing the merit of *Accounting Disrupted*. Robert Fox and Laura LeBlanc welcomed the idea and guided the contents, offering also the institute's vast resources for me to draw upon in writing the book. At Wiley, Sheck Cho has been immensely generous in providing advice on the structure and shape of the book and also ensuring that I was aware that time is of the essence!

I am thankful to the many who supported the project and helped me see how far digital technologies are impacting not just accounting and finance work and expertise but also organizations, economies, and our lives. I was fortunate to speak to many executives, decision makers, data scientists, IT leaders, entrepreneurs, finance managers, and accounting professionals, as well as students and business educators whose thoughts and ideas shaped my thinking. The insights captured here could not have been conceived without their inputs. A few individuals should be named, including Stelios Haji-Ionnou, Robert Hodgkinson, Warwick Hunt, Mo Ibrahim, Wol Kolade, Barry Melancon, Nick Read, Eric Ries, Martin Sorrell, Peter Thiel, Lance Uggla, and Adrian Wooldridge.

I thank my daughters, Lia and Sofiya, and my partner, Farah, for always being there.

About the Author

Al (Alnoor) Bhimani is a professor of Management Accounting and the director of the South Asia Centre at London School of Economics (LSE). He was previously head of LSE's Department of Accounting and inaugural director of LSE Entrepreneurship. His interests include financial management and digitization, strategic finance, and aspects of globalization, governance, and economic development. Al earned his BSc at King's College–London and an MBA from Cornell University, and he holds a PhD from LSE. He is also a CPA. He has written bestselling books dealing with accounting, financial management, technology, and digitalization. He sits on business school advisory boards in Africa, America, Europe, and Asia.

CHAPTER **1**

Accounting Disrupted

If you don't have the ability to navigate a new technology paradigm, you're not even going to be present for the future.[1]
—Satya Nadella, CEO, Microsoft

Unilever, the Anglo-Dutch owner of brands like Marmite, Ben & Jerry's, Dove, and Hellmann's, spends 14% of its revenues on brand and marketing. It recognizes the rapid change in its customers who are becoming more digitally savvy and exhibiting different values from past generations. Consumers who are technophiles and are especially concerned about the company's social and environmental impact are on the rise. Campaigns have to resonate with the changing habits and values of the customer base. To achieve this, the company leverages machine learning tools to segment consumers in terms of their preferences and based on this, uses programmatic, data-driven marketing to send them relevant messages via digital channels. Sensors are also embedded in every machine and building in order to provide digital representations of every process. This data is mined, and insights from AI systems and advanced analytics make possible predictions about quality concerns, malfunctions, and sustainability focused process issues. These automated systems enable Unilever to reach more customers in a targeted way, while reducing costs and freeing up employee resources to focus on other growth activities.

Alan Jope, Unilever's chief executive, notes that "the constraint is not money . . . but that the ability to manage the content-driven, highly targeted, data-led campaigns needs new people with new skills."[2] To ensure that there is full understanding of how resources, information, and customer changes are weaved into the digitalization drive, Unilever runs a long-term bonus scheme for senior executives with new metrics such as a "sustainability progress index" linked with "responsible digital marketing." Aside from cost savings and staying close to new generations of customers, digitally connecting marketing and production has allowed the company to launch new products much faster than it ever could in the past. Few issues tied to Unilever going digital remain outside the domain of finance.

Accountants believe that there is no business situation that accounting cannot report on. This is especially so when accounting reports integrate financial with nonfinancial information. From cost determinations to auditing, to taxation, to financial analyses, accounting information enables us to assess financial performance and to make business decisions. But accounting now faces a crunch – it needs to reshape itself from the core. The field has focused on reporting present and past economic transactions and business outcomes. Several disruptive trends are now in play that point to significant fissures in modern accounting expertise. For one, accounting information must start to speak to what will take place rather than on financial activities that have occurred. Also, executive action can increasingly be on autopilot such that financial objectives are pursued as if people were making decisions but where in fact there is no human input. So not only are forms and intents of accounting information changing but so are its readers. Further, although accounting usually reports on products passing through the value chain, we're seeing more and more situations where accounting itself becomes part of the products being reported on. Accounting is, in other words, becoming a whole lot more complex, and digitization is at the heart of the ongoing disruption.

What do digital technologies do? They enable businesses to convert physical (analog) text into *digitized* formats. As a consequence, enterprises alter their business models and work activities by *digitalizing* their processes. *Digital transformations* move enterprises into new realms of operating where all areas of business integrate digital technologies and a novel managerial culture takes effect. While accounting reports have always been about helping business decision-making, digitalization is unleashing a massive alteration as to what accounting now needs to achieve. This is because digital technologies have the power to self-transform and branch out to other sectors of the economy where productivity also increases. Technology hasn't always demonstrated such power. In fact, rarely so. We've only seen this happen three times before. The printing press did that about 600 years ago. So did the steam engine 300 years ago and the electric generator 200 years ago. Today, digital technologies are upending business philosophies, models, and thinking because they can self-transform. The pace and scale at which this is happening have no equal in history, and there's no technological U-turn. Accounting cannot afford to stand still. This book is about how accounting is being disrupted by digital technologies and the steps the field must take.

While digital technologies are impacting how we experience and consume things, the digital trajectories within business defy tradition in their capacity to supercharge economic growth. How has this come about? It is widely accepted that the First Industrial Revolution introduced mechanization about 250 years ago. Then, 150 years later, this was followed by electrification and mass production. Electronics and automation started a third revolution around 60 years ago. The ongoing and aptly termed Fourth Industrial Revolution sees our physical and virtual worlds converging. But this time it's different in that with the first three revolutions, few people understood the magnitude of changes taking place. However, today people are aware of the tectonic shifts that are impacting the way we produce, consume, move, communicate, and experience things. And we know businesses must act.

But there remains an unknown. In the past, managers introducing radical changes in their operations fully appreciated what they were seeking. It may have been an investment to increase productivity or to rebrand the product; or perhaps they sought to implement flexible work practices to enhance production flexibility and customer service. Or possibly, they desired a merger to acquire knowledge and mobilize new revenue streams. The paths advanced by decision makers could be deliberate, purposeful, and directive, leading to defined business outcomes. A digital transformation, however, can only offer a limited vision of what the end state might be. There exists no methodology to put into effect a digital maneuver that leads to a specific enduring outcome. In the digital world, the African fable must be heeded: Every morning a gazelle wakes up knowing it must run faster than the fastest lion or it will be killed and, every morning a lion wakes up knowing it must outrun the slowest gazelle or it will starve to death. Likewise, digitization begets digitization, following novel trajectories in the making. Any hindrance puts growth, if not survival, at risk. Where digital technologies are deployed, they alter processes, all the while triggering further changes that become essential but impossible to predict at the outset. While we are aware that we are living in a time of extreme economic renewal, we also know that undertaking fast iterative change is perforce the only approach that can be adopted. We cannot entirely fathom where digital paths will take us, but we know we have to react and be proactive, continually challenging the status quo. The question for us is what accounting now needs to do so we can forge effective advances given the extreme ruptures the digital economy is bringing. To better appreciate how accounting must be rethought, it is essential to ponder some wider global forces of change that businesses generally must address.

GLOBAL FORCES RESHAPING THE DIGITAL ECONOMY

In the next decade, the world's population will grow by a sixth. The United States population will rise by a meager 7.5% and that of Europe will decline by 2%. Moreover, 97% of the global population growth will be from the developing world and *Easternization* – the influencing habits and customs of fast-developing Asian countries – will march with high velocity. Of essence is that a third of Americans living in 2030 will have been born in the analog era. In the developing world, by contrast, 1.25 billion people will join the existing 6 billion and all will have been "born digital"! If digitization comes to equate with advancement, then Western developed nations will form a very tiny portion of tomorrow's advanced world.

Consider this: China and the United States are now the world's two largest economies. While China is called a *developing economy,* the United States is among the most advanced economies in the world. Put together, the two countries account for 90% of the market capitalization of the world's biggest digital platforms. They produce three-quarters of the world's patents tied to blockchain technologies and public cloud computing, and they account for half of the globe's Internet-of-Things expenditures. We may now speak of developing versus advanced economies, but digital technologies pay little heed to this differentiation. What matters is not where we've been but where we go from here. As such, China has more than 80% of its consumers using mobile payment systems, whereas in the United States, mobile payment apps have less than 10% adoption rates.[3] Digital systems are defining economic growth while discarding lead positions. Their usage seems neither aided nor hindered by how industrial history has shaped a nation. Managing as if yesterday mattered has no place in the digital world we have entered.

What does the ongoing technological shift not infiltrate? It turns out: very little. National programs of change and growth deeply entail digital transformations within every level of societal activity. It is anticipated that 70% of world economic value created in the next decade will have come from digitally enabled platforms.[4] Across the sustainable development goals (SDGs) supported by most nations as guides to the next decade's targets for peace and prosperity for people and the planet, digital developments will impact "virtually all the SDGs, and affect all countries, sectors and stakeholders," according to the UNCTAD's Digital Economy Report.[5]

It is, however, critical to understand that while the digital economy covers the globe, it does not do so in a consistent manner. Many emerging-market regions that have been slow to invest in complex industrial structures have hyper-digitalized economic segments that are leapfrogging advanced economy sectors. If there's little from the past to dismantle, then change can come about very swiftly. Antiquated systems in the advanced world prevail because it's difficult to justify replacing them with digitized systems. A case in point is M-Pesa, the mobile phone-based money transfer system developed in Kenya in 2007. M-Pesa has more registered accounts than Kenya has inhabitants, and the system moves over 50% of the country's GDP.[6] Conversely, in the West, mobile money movements on the scale of M-Pesa would be counter to institutionalized financial services founded on deeply established regulatory and governance structures. The excessive complexity of legacy systems, the lack of shared platforms, the extensive grip over consumers that credit cards enjoy, and the hardware cost hurdles to sellers all reduce the advent of mobile money. Inroads made by apps, such as Apple Pay, Google Pay, Samsung Pay, PayPal, Venmo, Square Cash, and Zelle, among others, dwarf similar systems in developing nations. This is because less well-grounded habits tied to the industrial economy help mobilize the transition over to digital products faster.

The relevance of demographic structures in the digital world extends much beyond just the significance of location and population size. While economic power will see alterations tied to population changes because of their nation-specific digital proclivities, so will the values and predilections of people by age group. We can expect that digitalization will entirely rewrite the social contract between people and business. This is happening already at an accelerated pace. But the reformulation of the social contract differs across age cohorts, where some are born digital versus analog. As a consequence, thought must be given to who defines accounting controls and for whom.

Consider that the next 10 years will see *Generation Xers* (usually classified as those born between 1960 and 1979) in the last third of their working life and looking to retirement. They grew up witnessing the rise of capitalism and systems of meritocracy and they benefited from opportunities not available to the previous generation. Competitiveness and individualism characterizes their mindset. Their predilection is for management systems that capture performance achievement within defined incentives and reward structures. Generation Xers who have succeeded veer toward the consumption of status labels, branded goods, and luxury articles. They tend to be the ones at the top of organizational hierarchies, setting the parameters by which enterprises operate. They will, for now, define the occupational experiences of *millennials* (those born roughly between 1980 and 1994) who are entering the 2020s at the ages of 25–40. This generation will have seen periods of general economic stability, the rise of globalization, and of course, the internet. Millennials have tended to be self-focused, thriving on experiences, interactions, experimentation, and travel. Their choices are not founded on lifelong loyalties or a desire for permanency of any sort. Management systems they react to are ones that are quick and clear about how positive performance is tied to immediate returns.

A good proportion of *Generation Zers* (born between 1995–2010) are today just entering the workforce. Their perspective is shaped by an era of mobility and wide social networks. They are the true digital natives, perceiving the analog world at best as quaint but in fact incomprehensible. They desire uniqueness, which they like to communicate to large communities of people, and they subscribe to a citizenship of ethics and analytical legitimacy that favors authenticity, acceptance, and openness to different kinds of people and ways of being. For them, self-expression trumps the desire to fit in. Their forte lies in the evaluation of large amounts of information, which makes them *identity nomads*.[7] Having only narrow stakeholder representation is not something Generation Zers support. They will not tolerate businesses that lean toward any element of machoism or that discriminate on the grounds of difference. They favor ones that treat products more as services that connect consumers. In the digital age, Zers require unique enterprise strategies and financial assessments that differ from those that industrial organizations nurtured. Greater fragmentation of channels, increased connectivity between individuals and firms, and a respect for truthfulness as well as plurality of ideals all make for altered approaches to the management of Generation Z workers. A clash of perspectives between those who celebrate Industrial Age values and those who exhibit digitally grounded propensities can hinder business growth. Financial controls deployed in enterprises need to align with the groupings of culture within the workforce, especially as people live and work longer.

Another key element of changing demographics is the increasing participation of women in workplaces. In developed economies, women play a far from equal but still rapidly growing role as workers across all industrial sectors. While gender disparities continue to exist, the proportion of women in technology and startups is increasing apace. This is positively changing business and the functioning of organizations. Digital transformations open new avenues for the economic empowerment of women with digital platforms, mobile phones, and digital financial services enabling *leapfrogging* possibilities for women to increase their employment opportunities, and access knowledge and general information.[8] Accounting systems will need to adjust, not simply in identifying and monitoring inclusivity, but also in adjusting to alternative directions and business model innovations that contrast with male-oriented enterprise control structures. In the developing world, the expected population increase of women digital natives in the next decade will exceed 3.6 billion. The World Bank reports that digital technologies and new online platforms will create opportunities for women to bypass traditional work and trade barriers, expand their entrepreneurial skills, and, where social-cultural norms dictate, enable them to develop flexible careers allowing work and household responsibilities to be better managed.[9] A study across 30 countries reveals a growing number of women enrolling in higher education institutions across the Muslim world where traditionally, women representation suffered extensively.[10] Evidence is mounting that women in all nations are leveraging opportunities and the flexibility offered by digital technologies both as workers and as consumers. Women's educational adeptness combined with the potential digital technologies offer combined with the global drive to balance gender inequities will inevitably alter the workings of business. Accounting systems will have to concurrently revise the premise of their own workings.

What takes place in business enterprises is influenced by the education employees have received. But to what extent is formal business education preparing us for the digitally transformed organization? Business academics regrettably remain, in the main, largely in the dark as to what is appropriate management education for the digital era. When the world's first business school was set up over 200 years ago in France, agricultural work was shifting to industrial production activities. In the United States, Wharton began teaching business 140 years ago and Harvard established the world's first MBA program in 1907. At the time, the largest industrial structures the world had ever seen were being mounted. Initially, business education was grounded in practice. Industrialists and functional managers were interviewed and the detailed accounts of what they did were transformed into case studies for discussion by business students. This worked well until the 1960s when business school professors felt the desire for academic distinction in the eyes of other scholars. This was a time that saw the rise of digital processes via semiconductors, computing and later the internet. But business schools eschewed practice-focused professional management training, opting instead for the scientific model espoused by academia.[11] Present-day business school professors have not moved far from economic theorizing that piggybacks on scientific principles, which they purport define effective management education.

We're now seeing the deployment of robotics, miniature sensors, artificial intelligence, genetic sequencing, and 4D printing, which demand an altered understanding of their business potential, while business school educators remain wedded to advancing academic research founded on ideas about management education that are six decades old. Does this matter? It matters a great deal! As digitalization moves literally at the speed of light, accounting practices will need to meet the needs of decision makers who seek business-grounded solutions. Both accounting information and the analysis of such information will have to be suitable for executive needs that we have not seen before. Digitalization may be blind to how we define economic development, but it won't be subservient to educational lacunas.

WHAT DO BUSINESSES WANT?

What business would not want to benefit from greater productivity, a larger range of diverse products and services, heightened quality, and reduced costs? Business objectives such as these are ingrained in the psyche of industrial era managers. Digitalization goes beyond this. As we progress into a digitally transformed business world, the question needs to be asked: Should we limit pursued outcomes to only those that correspond to our current understanding of how businesses operate? Traditionally, we have regarded the existence of predictable repetitive tasks as a reason for investing in automation and digital technologies so that the efficiency of production can be enhanced. While the reduction of costs is laudable, this objective is dwarfed by the value to be derived from a significantly different strategic direction, which digitalization helps maneuver a business into. The capacity to understand and leverage what digital technologies can bring is essential but also markedly different from Industrial Age managerial pursuits.

How confident are enterprises that they can navigate the digital era whilst following their existing modus operandi? In one survey of 2,000 companies, 92% believed themselves to have business models that would not be economically viable as digitalization takes hold. Half of finance leaders believe their expertise does not have the right mix of capabilities to meet future priorities.[12] While fundamental economic logic must prevail, the mechanics of how this logic plays out in the face of digital technology usage is not well understood. If we assume that digitalization offers just operational change possibilities, we will have missed the point about its value in connecting and propelling more grounded and continuous engagements between people and structures. Digital processes enable and require a different form of analytics that is at variance with accounting's conventional reporting. Predictive engagement of a type not accessible before is part of the digital circuitry. An executive mindset that comprehends evolved business models that eschew traditional business trade-offs has become essential.

Decision makers have to tackle difficult new questions that have cropped up. Business executives recognize that demand and supply always need to be understood to work out the price at which transactions clear. But given that fixed costs have altered markedly and marginal costs are close to zero and that many cross-connections are in place, what cost management fundamentals should one resort to? And where digital exchanges can help make sense of what customers seek before any financial exchanges takes place, how do we account for the growth in value for firms that better match product offerings to customer desires in the absence of economic transactions? We know also that digital products can consolidate product offerings into solo devices where traditionally, a multitude of separate products would have been the norm. A smartphone is a camera, a map, a thesaurus, a game console, and more. How do we then deal with market sales points where traditional industry product boundaries are crossed? Simply looking for the point of price clearance according to conventional management folklore can no longer work. Grasping a wider vision of the potential of digitalization requires transcending the confines we've placed around industrial firm logic.

Applying a digital management mindset necessitates a fundamental change in our decision-making approaches. Sound executive action used to imply that small incremental changes should be pursued and feedback obtained to analyze the impact. Such feedback would then inform the next iteration within a steady path of action. In current digital contexts, the only safe path is one that is radical and transformational. What would have been regarded as a strategically effective move to be undertaken over a protracted time frame conventionally would today more likely have to be swift action that triggers further near-term deep action.

WITH GREAT DATA POWER COMES GREAT RESPONSIBILITY

All enterprises today are, to a degree, tech companies. Data can power their growth in whatever sector they may be in. In fact, information processing capacity has its place alongside other core competitive strengths within organizations to feed through performance. In essence, all companies must seek to develop capabilities to process and extract intelligence from data to advance their evolving business models. But many factors impinge on the process through which data is capable of effectively driving decisions and value creation. Maintaining the sanctity of data is essential. Data risk across the global business community is rising and cyber-breaches are on a growth path. The 2019 CEO Imperative Study that surveyed 200 CEOs from the Americas, Europe, the Middle East, Africa, and the Asia-Pacific region identified cybersecurity breaches as the biggest threat to the global economy.[13] Information that has high decision usefulness is also subject to very high levels of risk. Educating workers as to sound digital habits is important for enterprises as human errors and the nonobservance of security protocols result in expensive system failure costs. Moreover, valuable data can require input from humans who are dispersed. Information drawn from different places can be particularly useful but dispersion of data collection also increases the potential of breaches.

The focus of accounting systems has conventionally been premised on controls associated with recording economic transactions. Such controls provide assurance about the information collected. But where data of relevance is not captured through conventional financial records, information system controls must evolve to provide the same level of assurance. This enhances the need for awareness by the finance function as to data sources which are outside the usual parameters of control. Finance professionals need to expand their conception of enterprise control in firms that go digital. Security and assurance is essential in a world of growing business digitalization where cyber-resilience is of supreme importance.

Aside from information security and assurance requirements, regulatory limits are being placed about what data may be accessed by firms and their applicable uses. There is a shift away from the extraction and ownership of data to an environment where data is entrusted by those who produce it and is "borrowed" temporarily. As more widespread data regulations and compliance requirements take effect, accounting practices will have to continuously reflect legal framework changes. Digital data usage departs from the simplicity of recording and examining financial transactions-derived data that are unproblematically captured and owned by enterprises. As data analyses and processes lead to enterprise action that extends the scope for customer personalization, novel modes of trust and security compliance are emerging. For instance, new systems of reviews and ratings are coming into existence. Such emerging information sources will increasingly need to be part of accounting reports. Additionally, where audit and independent verifications are essential, the scope of evidence will have to widen significantly to encompass different sources of data. The finance function will need to invest into understanding the role of digital technologies that both produce different information types to investigate and that also help in verification protocols to aid compliance.

WHY DATA IS GROWING

Over 40 years ago, Bill Gates wanted to see a computer on every desk in every home. This produced a lot of data – much of which remained within devices. With music, games, movies, and files becoming digital, data transfers grew. Initially, much of the transfers were in one direction, but then exchanges could take place, creating more data. Today, digital devices enable value to be created through interfacing networks and the widening of connections. Such connections are, to some extent, triggered by people using those devices. But much more so, smart devices exponentially increase data exchanges through interconnections between devices. For instance, *citizen-to-citizen* data stems from social media and communications via devices that already connect half the world's population. *Business-to-consumer* channels also create data via media, services, and consumer activities. *Business-to-business* interfacing growingly expands global value chain processes and enterprise activities, including personnel and financial data operations. Another growing source of data is also *government-to-citizen* services. All these connections are producing data at an accelerating pace. In the next five years, three-quarters of the world's population will be digitally connected and will therefore create avalanches of data.

Where in the world is data growing most? As noted earlier, population growth will largely accrue to the developing world going forward. Five years ago, the United States, China, Europe, the Middle East, and Africa were about at par in terms of digital data production. By 2025, the United States' share will be much smaller than that of China, Europe, and the Asia-Pacific (including Japan but excluding China). During that time, the world will see a fourfold increase in data produced!

While people using devices create data, the biggest source of data production today comes from embedded devices that enable machine-to-machine exchanges. The internet of things (IoT) comprises the network of physical devices, machines, vehicles, and a myriad of other items with embedded sensors like RFID readers, chip cards, smart meters, medical implants, security cameras, cellular networks, traffic grids, and others that invoke interactions that continuously produce growing swathes of data. Such data, if effectively harnessed, can provide avenues that allow businesses to produce greater value. Intelligent systems that may be under the purview of the finance function can give insights into trends and possibilities, generate adaptive responses, customize user experiences in real time, and deliver deep analytics. Harnessing and analyzing data generated by connectivities can offer intelligence never before accessible, which can feed continuously into decision-making processes.

New data forms can further permeate the wider supply chain of processes and quickly point to new strategic possibilities. As noted, this is a result of digital technologies being able to self-transform and extend to other segments of the economy where productivity increases results. In this sense, more data leads to more data creation. The finance function, as we'll see in later chapters, will add to this by producing data about data. Such digital data can be used and reformatted for further use and can be moved, processed, and copied quickly and cheaply, thereby enabling decisions that could not be pondered before, and help design new products and pursue alternative courses of business action. Very importantly, data is not just a product but also a byproduct whose utility can be extracted.

The rise of digital data is growing across several dimensions. The *volume* of data growth far exceeds what could be produced by

the number of digital devices on the planet because interconnections between these devices and other digital mechanisms propel
data growth exponentially. But the speed at which data is produced is
also rising. Partly, speed of not just growth but also of exchanges and
access increases the possibilities for data's use. The increased *velocity*
of data production can be of particular value say for efficient traffic
flow management, especially where vehicles are becoming "smarter."
Prioritizing traffic pathways for emergency response vehicles, direct-
ing real-time fraud detection through facial recognition as security
mechanisms, medical diagnostics processes, and so on, all benefit
from the speed of data transfers. By 2025, a quarter of the world's
data will be accessed and used to add real-time value, and most of
it will come from IoT devices. One in five human activities will then
rely critically on data exchanges taking place once every 18 seconds
per person.[14] Within industry, production processes will also rely on
data exchanges. For instance, predictive maintenance can be enabled
through IoT technologies whereby sensors track the condition of
machines and facilities, continuously sending data to a cloud application using communication networks. This triggers assessments of
maintenance requirements, which ensure shorter downtimes, greater
production efficiency, and lower production costs.

Data is only structured if steps are taken to make it so. But much
data utility derives from semi-structured and unstructured forms
of data that can be processed for managerial purposes. The quality of
data being analyzed needs to be high to ensure its usefulness. Data
made into information that is meaningful and valuable must encompass *veracity* before being fed into trust-reliant activities such as safety
measure warnings, medical condition tracking, and so on. We'll see
in later chapters that finance professionals need to understand issues
of variety, quality, and speed, aside from volume impact tied to digital
data growth and usage.

IF FINANCE STANDS STILL

In a world of changing risks, growing data, enhanced digitization, and
increased regulations, no finance leader can afford to stand still. Digital
technologies are impacting the way finance operates, what it reports

on, and how it helps the organization. The automation and standardization of accounting activities across enterprises has been ongoing for a long time and is continuing. Today robotic-based process automation is taking the lead within finance operations to enhance error-free work, produce faster reports, and ensure verifiability – all at a lower cost. This does replace humans engaged in repetitive tasks with technologies that can perform better and faster at lower costs. Additionally, software-as-a-service and cloud-based systems likewise continue to enable financial management processes to maintain currency and remain effective at a lower cost. Capital expenditures tend to convert into operating expenses which alter the structure of financial statements. Such technologies can help ensure enterprises remain flexible and sensitive to innovations but require the right digital technology skills in the workforce and cyber-resilience and security systems being invested into.

More fundamental changes than automation in the finance function relate to the application of advanced analytics. Organizations need to process and analyze large amounts of structured and unstructured data to extract forward-looking insights. Big data platforms can be interrogated via machine-learning tools, and patterns and trends can be assessed to track through developments that present market opportunities or rising risks or evolving customer preferences, and so on. As Vincent dell'Anno of EY notes: ". . . you want to facilitate analytics as close to the source of data as possible, you want to be able to drive streaming analytics where possible that are relevant to the business problem."[15] Additionally, artificial intelligence (AI) can help detect new patterns and adapt to emerging conditions, including altered accounting reporting standards and changing tax rates and regulations and offer recommendations or support advice developed by accountants. Blockchains (discussed in Chapter 2) will likewise assist with contracts, enhance security and increase value chain efficacy.

So what must finance executives do differently with the changes these digital technologies are bringing? It must be accepted that organizations require keeping a focus on accounting reports, budgetary controls, and funds flow reporting. This is unlikely to change. However, these processes will be supplemented by new ones and in time, possibly diminish in scope. When organizations make investments, kneejerk controls kick in. Projects have to be justified on the basis of costs and revenues or savings. Where insights derive from a wider array of data that is analyzed part by humans and part digital systems including accountants and AI agents, indicators may point to the need for funds to be allocated based on trends that are not reliant solely on economic transactions, but on evolving ones. The input of accounting information into organizational processes will, for now, retain elements of what has conventionally been asked of the finance function, but digitalization will make it necessary that the work of accountants also evolves.

Enterprise growth has always depended on an ability to differentiate a business from the competition. This will be a mounting requirement as markets become increasingly digitized. The ability to merely understand what produces data and their different forms will not suffice for accounting executives to deliver value. An understanding of novel business models, made possible by digital technologies and knowing how to capture insights and hidden knowledge about the organizational environment, including intelligence on competitors, suppliers, customers, and structural market changes, must feature as evolving competitive strengths if the profession is to survive. The time is now for the finance function to bring to decision makers an understanding of the disruption that digital technologies are causing and the many opportunities they open up. The production of relevant information has always been part of accounting work, and accounting executives will have to learn to play a role in enabling embedded analytics whereby machine agents capture and organize data within business activities that require informed human input. In the emerging digital economy, the accountant will have to nurture the capacity for information production from data sources to positively engage business. If the finance professional does not take this on, accounting's usefulness will dwindle into insignificance in the years to come.

NOTES

1. Nadella, S., and Eucher, J. 2018. *Navigating Digital Transformation*. Research-Technology Management 61 (4): p. 11–15.
2. Spanier, G. 2019. *Unilever saves €500m as in-housing is 'more efficient' than agencies*. https://www.campaignlive.co.uk/article/unilever-saves-%E2%82%AC500m-in-housing-more-efficient-agencies/1578798

3. Toit, G., Bradley, K., Swinton, S., Murns, M., and Gooyer, C. 2018. *In Search of Customers Who Love their Bank.*

4. World Economic Forum. 2020. Shaping the future of digital economy and new value creation. https://www.weforum.org/platforms/shaping-the-future-of-digital-economy-and-new-value-creation

5. World Economic Forum. 2019. Our shared digital future: Responsible digital transformation – board briefing. White paper (February 6). https://www.weforum.org/whitepapers/our-shared-digital-future-responsible-digital-transformation-board-briefing-9ddf729993

6. Rolfe, A. 2019. *Mobile money transaction equivalent of half of Kenya's GDP.* https://www.paymentscardsandmobile.com/mobile-money-transactions-half-of-kenyas-gdp/

7. Francis, T. and Hoefel, F. 2018. *'True Gen': Generation Z and its implications for companies.* https://www.mckinsey.com/industries/consumer-packaged-goods/our-insights/true-gen-generation-z-and-its-implications-for-companies

8. OECD. 2018. Bridging The Digital Gender Divide. http://www.oecd.org/internet/bridging-the-digital-gender-divide.pdf

9. World Bank. 2020. Women and Trade. https://www.worldbank.org/en/topic/trade/publication/women-and-trade-the-role-of-trade-in-promoting-womens-equality

10. Zahidi, S. 2018. *Fifty Million Rising.* New York: Nation Books.

11. Bennis, W., and Toole, J. 2005. How business schools lost their way. *Harvard Business Review* 96 (5): 96–104, 154.

12. Fitzpatrick, M. 2020. *The Digital-Led Recovery From Covid-19: Five Questions for CEOs.* https://www.Mckinsey.Com/Business-Functions/Mckinsey-Digital/Our-Insights/The-Digital-Led-Recovery-From-Covid-19-Five-Questions-For-Ceos#

13. Klimas, T. 2019. DNA of the CFO: Is the future of finance new technology or new people? *EY* (April 11). https://www.ey.com/en_gl/advisory/is-the-future-of-finance-new-technology-or-new-people

14. Taylor, C. 2019. *Cybersecurity is the biggest threat to the world economy over the next decade, CEOs say.* CNBC (July 9). https://www.cnbc.com/2019/07/09/cybersecurity-biggest-threat-to-world-economy-ceos-say.html

15. Klimas, DNA of the CFO: Is the future of the finance new technology or new people?

CHAPTER **2**

Unleashing Digitization

In today's era of volatility, there is no other way but to re-invent. The only sustainable advantage you can have over others is agility, that's it.[1]
—Jeff Bezos, CEO, Amazon.com

When Mark Matthews, head of operations for the corporate bank, investment bank, and capital release units at Deutsche Bank, put the bank on the path to digital, he knew digitalizing work would improve services and help positively change the work culture by facilitating cross-functional cooperation. His team initially created activity and organizational maps and costing models across all functions and then looked at how to bridge the mini-ecosystems operating across the bank. One outcome of going digital was to increase accuracy and speed of work through robotic process automation (RPA) where desktop-based digital helper apps assisted with repetitive tasks automation. The RPA applications mimicked what humans did by undertaking tasks at scale in a controlled, approved manner. In some areas, 30–70% of processes became automated reducing employee training time extensively. The RPA tools also enabled the bank to streamline manual aspects of money-laundering process checks, saving 210,000 hours of checking work that humans would have performed. The automation process checked more than 3.4 million positions and automatically closed 380,000 accounts.

Aside from RPA systems (RPAs), the bank operationalized unattended intelligent automation where machines perform tasks and make decisions on their own. This was undertaken via artificial intelligence tools that scanned news sentiment and context for negative news, managing to half the time it took employees to screen clients for adverse media that was a part of the bank's know-your-customer screening processes. The bank's digitalization efforts extended to using SalesForce. com as its customer-relationship management platform, which was coupled with machine learning software for client management. The blended system enables Deutsche Bank personnel to identify potential customer issues and resolve them before they actualize into problems.[2]

For decades, we've come to regard accounting as a process of identifying, measuring, and communicating economic information so users of this information can make informed judgments and decisions.[3] Eyeing just economic information to make decisions is misplaced, and seeing accounting in such terms today is in fact antiquated! Of course, finance teams cannot yet completely move away from timely closure of the books, or plan forecasts and prepare budgets, or produce standardized and accurate reports and cost analyses. But it's clear that digitalization is transforming how enterprises operate, and as novel technologies generate greater depth, breadth, and variety of data in ways we've not seen before, finance has to reinvent itself. Going digital is upending industrial structures and creating new business models that sustain products, services, and ways of working that until recently could not have been conceived. What's more, current corporate models are beginning to acknowledge that digitalization presents few boundaries. It affects every supply chain node and every activity point tied to internal operations. Digitalization impacts vertically integrated enterprise models as much as outsourcers. Little can escape the effects of digital. This places an urgent onus on finance executives to rethink the processes by which they can add value, as well as the skills through which to do so.

New challenges for finance include the transitioning, if not the emergence of entirely new business models, delivering real-time on-the-go reporting, tackling emerging governance demands, extending, and upgrading the ITC knowledge base, tightening cybersecurity, and rebalancing the workforce's hard/soft skills mix. These are tall orders but not ones that can be ignored let alone delayed. We discuss these and other implications of digitalization in subsequent chapters but consider here the major classes of new digital technologies that are impacting accounting work. A number of digital applications such as blockchain technology (BT), robotic process automation (RPA), artificial intelligence (AI), machine learning, and others are affecting many areas of accounting work and financial control. What's more, interdependencies between these technologies are growing as the digital transformation landscape becomes more complex and more interactive. We need to understand the building blocks of digital enterprise transformations to work out what in finance must change. We'll do that here by first asking, why change anything?

WHY IS FINANCE CHANGING?

It's clear enterprises feel compelled to invest in digital technologies that are reshaping how they function. The implications are many. Executive decision-making has always relied on financial information input and, as we'll see, that input has to tally with what digitalization alters. Finance leaders must now focus on what is taking place in business environments and the opportunities that are opening up for the enterprises they serve, as well as address challenges which market environments pose based on deeper interpretations of external signals. Simply delivering historical financial data on a periodic basis can no longer be their primary role. Additionally, accounting work is itself being transformed. The automation of traditional accounting activities implies that a huge volume of transactions can be processed using less resources in less time. This must be a welcome development as between half and three-quarter of accountants' time is spent on repetitive low value tasks.[4] Many companies find that workflow software can drive down the volume of repetitive tasks such as collating financial data from different company units into one general ledger, processing invoices, preparing reconciliations, and gathering data for compliance with accounting standards and corporate regulations. These changes, once successfully undertaken within one part of the business, increase automation expertise that can be applied across other parts of the enterprise.

We can think of yesterday's accounting focus as entailing the collection of data based on economic transactions and related quantitative and qualitative metrics where the aim has been to produce financial reports for managers to act on (see Figure 2.1).

Finance executives in digitally transforming firms are becoming more implicated in determining cloud infrastructure benefits; managing process changes and their costs; assessing cybersecurity issues; and leading debates on flexibility, automation, and scalability. Their role is not only more intense in terms of data sources growth but also in becoming more cross-functional, where enhanced reporting and

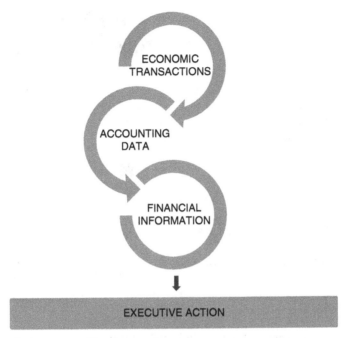

Figure 2.1 Traditional accounting.

the movement toward data-driven decisions and the application of rules-based automation cut across the activities of enterprises.

Data derived from outside the domain of economic transactions help more comprehensively identify current trends and provide intelligence on novel possibilities for action and opportunities for growth. This translates into activities that machines can undertake and continuously learn from – activities that also provide information and insights for assessment that other executives can harness and deploy. Finance teams are, in other words, becoming changemakers going far beyond providing just efficiency expertise, because machines can assist in taking care of certain actions based on data inputs and subsequently they can refine these actions based on data from prior actions (see Figure 2.2). In parallel, humans can focus on using information to determine actions they decide to concentrate on which also produces yet more data for analysis.[5]

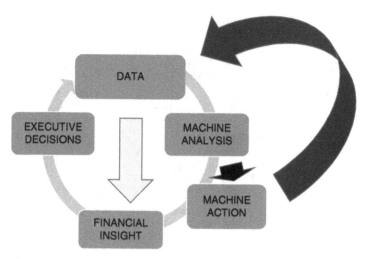

Figure 2.2 Accounting in digitalizing enterprises.

THE RISE OF DIGITAL

It's clear that data plays a big role with both machines and individuals taking actions, which generate yet more data that subsequently drive more actions. Lack of awareness of the potential offered by new technologies is the single biggest obstacle to advancing the finance function. But what specific technologies are altering finance? The largest investments that have been undertaken across digitalizing firms include advanced analytics systems, machine learning, optical character recognition, artificial intelligence, robotic process automation, and distributed ledger technology. These and other technologies discussed below are not only altering enterprise processes, models, and products but also making the finance function less transactional and more focused on value provision.

BLOCKCHAIN TECHNOLOGY

Blockchain's principal hurdle right now is that there is little cognizance of its capacity to alter enterprise functions and to date, most of the adoption has been in the financial industry, though other sectors are seeing an increased number of applications. Just how seriously should accounting experts take blockchain technologies? It is well acknowledged that "general purpose technologies" have changed the world. Examples are the steam engine that unleashed industrialism, railroads that enabled the rise of department stores and propelled the growth of central business districts, the automobile which sponsored the spread of shopping centers, and the internet, which triggered a whole new paradigm for economic value creation. We have entered the *fourth industrial era* that sees the physical, virtual, and biological worlds merging and where the interactions linking them will simultaneously increase the need for what blockchain systems can deliver.

A blockchain system itself can be regarded as a general purpose technology.[6] Indeed, blockchains are giving rise to novel business models, and like the steam engine, trains, automobiles, and the internet, they will alter preexisting economic and social structures and transform societies. The possibilities blockchains offer business are huge. The World Economic Forum suggests that 10% of global GDP could be stored on blockchains by 2025. Ignoring the capacity of blockchains to reshape enterprise processes will sponsor corporate downfalls – a mishap that cannot be allowed of finance.

So what is a blockchain? In terms digestible to accountants, it is a data structure that enables digital records of transactions to be created and shared across a distributed network of computers. For this reason, BT is also referred to as distributed ledger technology. Significantly, any network user can add to the ledger without having to liaise with a centralized authority. One way of thinking of blockchain's modus operandi has been nicely described as follows:

> You (a "node") have a file of transactions on your computer (a "ledger"). Two government accountants (let's call them "miners") have the same file on theirs (so it's "distributed"). As you make a transaction, your computer sends an e-mail to each accountant to inform them.

> Each accountant rushes to be the first to check whether you can afford it (and be paid their salary "Bitcoins"). The first to check and validate hits "REPLY ALL," attaching their logic for verifying the transaction ("proof of work"). If the other accountant agrees, everyone updates their file . . .[7]

BT can serve as a pragmatic solution to business problems across industrial sectors from financial institutions, to health care organizations, as well as firms in transportation, retail, merchandising, and manufacturing as well as the supply chains they underpin. A growing number of enterprises are deploying blockchain systems. Walmart is an early adopter, as are Dole, Tyson, and Nestle, principally because of the advantages offered in enabling robust records to be kept. Walmart, for instance, uses blockchains to keep track of the pork from China that the company sources, whereby identifiers are maintained as to from where each meat piece has been sourced – including its processing, storage, and expiry date. Likewise, De Beers, the diamond behemoth, deploys blockchains for tracking precious stones from their mining point through their processing and sale to the customer. The records help the company manage issues of blood diamonds and ownership.

Generally, companies adopting blockchain cite various advantages including developing new business models, altering value chains, achieving greater security and lower risk, and increasing the speed of organizational activities. According to a Deloitte survey,[8] the question for executives is no longer "Will blockchain work?" but "How can we make blockchain work for us?" As a ledger technology, a blockchain system can address the needs of financial transactions relating to payments tied to trading, settlements, and pay-outs; and it can connect to smart contracts that automatically execute agreed upon transactions when specified conditions are met.

Blockchain can be applied to numerous recordkeeping tasks. A property sale transaction requiring, say, a mortgage, can be managed via a blockchain application where documents from different parties are collected and processed in a manner that replicates what would have previously been done by different agents (sales agents, lawyers, loan officers, surveyors, regulators, etc.). In effect, any contract, certification, proof of ownership, or right of use including linkages tied to supply chain nodes – can be purposefully tracked via blockchain mechanisms. They can be applied to pretty much any existing finance-related process including payments, planning, lending and funding, trading and investment, insurance, cybersecurity, operations, and communications.

It is likely that within a short period of time, product identifiers, medical, academic, and other records, and all contexts where trust is being brokered by intermediaries (bankers, insurers, notaries, etc.) will move to blockchain applications. This implies a shift in the corporate and organizational mind-set. Naturally, as executives transition from conventional mechanical modes of assurance toward more efficacious digital ones where trust is baked into the technology, the redesign of the finance function will follow suit.

Blockchains can drive productivity increases, ensure transparency, and reduce time and paper inefficiencies. Additionally, they can better service consumers by meeting needs that have been overlooked. This naturally opens the door for enterprises to extend the product range they can offer and indeed point to new business models. In terms of increasing revenues, streamlining processes, reducing supply chain inefficiencies, and general cost cutting, blockchains' greatest impacts are in the automotive, telecommunications, tech-media, health care, and the public sectors, alongside property, insurance, financial services, and the agricultural sectors. The direct impact on public accounting are also immense. The entire justification for conventional audits may even be pondered given that the immutability and assurance embedded in blockchain technologies is the premise on which audits are justified. Where there are numerous transacting parties, blockchains overcome the requirement to reconcile disparate ledgers as well as the expense that might be entailed in having a central authority ensuring the accuracy of the ledger. Those with access to the ledger can trace all prior transactions that have taken place, which heightens transparency and in a sense enables the blockchain to represent the core of the audit aim itself. Where BT deployment carries across business chains, the justification for conventional audit-based forms of verification subsides. This is further discussed in Chapter 6.

What are the hurdles that blockchains currently face? Business transactions entail costs of *verification* where attributes need to be checked, for instance when goods move through a supply chain. They also give rise to *networking* costs where resources need to be expanded to establish and maintain a business relationship. Blockchain systems can drastically lower these two business costs.[9] The hurdles that

BT implementation face are dwarfed in relation to these two costs, which finance executives will have on their radar. Enterprises considering the deployment of blockchains also see regulatory issues as a key challenge to adopting the technology. Additionally, many firms looking to implement blockchain applications require joining other organizations and possibly interfacing with competitors to set up or to become part of viable consortia, which can be met with resistance. Lack of in-house capabilities and uncertain returns on investment (ROIs) in relation to costs and payoffs pose further BT adoption challenges – all of which point to the need for involvement of the finance function.

If a blockchain is public, then by definition every transaction recorded can be visible to anyone. This raises issues of ethics, security, and compliance where there is availability of information in the public domain. Organizations can opt to keep their blockchain systems *permissioned* or *private* like an intranet. In contrast to permissionless systems, private blockchains can be accessed only by those who are provided authorization from a central authority. The central authority determines the governance structure of the blockchain. This enables close monitoring of compliance with regulations and more robust control over data.

A private blockchain can extend between business units or corporate groups or entities across a supply chain where there are frequent transactions. Major expenses can be avoided because once central authorities such as banks, clearinghouses, and lawyers are replaced, the unique ledger is accessible to all permissioned users and there is no need for reconciliations. Cost savings accrue from the centralized system that self-reconciles across parties. The trust embedded in the system also makes decision-making quicker as verification requirements do not hamper business. Further, where appropriate, regulators, tax authorities, and other oversight bodies can be given viewing rights to the blockchain to enable real-time monitoring. As such, the implications for accounting and finance professionals are extensive. They cannot shy away from the direction of travel that blockchain presents.

Security threats are important to consider in the light of what blockchain can offer. Although it is difficult to argue that blockchain systems are completely secure – "No one has yet managed to break the encryption and decentralized architecture of a blockchain"[10] – still, blockchains today represent a divergent technology where multiple protocols and standards are being developed. Over time there will be some harmonization of standards, as is the case with most new technologies, and some industry leaders will emerge. Of importance is that BT may give "the impression that it's a self-secured technology. This could not be further from the truth."[11] This is because blockchains get built on top of equipment and networks that themselves need to be secure to begin with. If this is not the case, blockchain systems will just mask preexisting security flaws. Accountants fully understand the notion of "garbage in – garbage out." Recognizing this in relation to the potential and limits of the evolving blockchain tech-space is a must.

ROBOTIC PROCESS AUTOMATION

Robotic process automation is a key step in the automation path organizations pursue. About a third of total task hours in the workplace are today carried out by machines though this is rapidly rising. RPA is accelerating the trend where enterprises replicate the tasks carried out by human workers through software robots that are programmed such that they can enter into applications, retrieve data, undertake calculations, and instructions and once the task is complete they log out. RPAs in doing this, automate structured and rule-based tasks. Regarded as software tools to integrate applications to automate routine predictable tasks using structured automation data, RPAs do not generally mobilize intelligence.

Differing levels of RPA sophistication exist. *Probots* follow simple, repetitious rules. *Knowbots* can collect and store user focused information and *chatbots* operate as virtual assistants capable of interacting with user queries in real time. RPAs are not intelligent in that they do not adjust to changes or make decisions other than mimicking human actions and working through codified rules that trigger predefined software reactions. RPAs can be operationalized to sit atop a firm's existing IT system without change in the infrastructure. If new parameters of data are to be introduced, the RPA must be restructured. Some enterprises seeing the benefits of RPA systems incorporate learning capabilities where RPAs get converted into intelligent process automation agents that are able to learn and get closer to simulating human behavior. In essence, they enter the realm of artificial intelligence.

There exist over 50 RPA software vendors whose offerings are continuously evolving. The 10 largest vendors account for around 70% of the market.[12] The key reasons for implementing RPA technologies are to optimize operational efficiency, accelerate existing processes, and to optimize costs. The business disruption and novel modes of remote working triggered by the COVID-19 pandemic are leading many organizations to consider using RPA as a tactical automation option to digitize paper-based, routine human processes.

ARTIFICIAL INTELLIGENCE

Artificial intelligence is artificial only to the degree that it is the product of human intelligence, but it can in many ways be smarter than people. AI refers to machines that are capable of performing tasks and making decisions that ordinarily require human intelligence. Humans can learn, reason, recognize things, and sometimes correct themselves! Artificial intelligence accords the same qualities to machines, which then can replace humans in undertaking these tasks. The capacity to learn from data access not exhibited by standard RPAs is referred to as *machine learning* – a subset of artificial intelligence with a focus on structured data. In essence, the intent is to have algorithms that get machines to look at historical data, reclassify that data, recognize patterns, and generate auto-corrective behavior in an attempt to drive organizational performance. Machine learning may require humans to intermittently reconfigure computing structures through altered code.

Large volumes of data can be analyzed via machine learning systems with patterns being uncovered all the while with learning taking place. This then contributes to decision-making that is comparable to human thinking. Predictive texting and product recommending systems are examples. A subset of machine learning is *deep learning*, which focuses on unstructured and abstract data. Tagging in social media relies on deep learning where categorization is based on comparisons with large and similar data sets. More than just mimicking human thinking, some machines are able to exhibit "superintelligence" and surpass human cognitive ability. Deep learning can bring this about where layers of complexity include high-level abstractions, which then drill down to specific features that become more useful. Ultimately, AI can derive learnings from structured data that comprises much of conventional accounting information supplementing this with unstructured data such as images and text.

BIG DATA ANALYTICS

Digital technologies are founded on improvements in the capacity to exchange data. But the value of information lies in analysis, and AI systems can underpin big data analysis. To users of digital tools, the value may lie in the delivery of specific services that meet defined consumer needs such as creating desirable experiences and enabling tasks to be carried out. Fundamental to their operations, all digital technologies produce data that can create extreme value if effectively harnessed. Ultimately, information is what drives decision-making, and digitalization produces such massive amounts of data – which, for good reason, we refer to as *big data* – that growing ways to connect information drawn from big data analysis to enabling decision-making enhancement must be of value to every organization. Big data includes traditional data forms that are numeric or text-based, but much more than this, big data also encompasses *unstructured* data derived from exchanges between communication platforms and devices, including video clips, audio data, and others. *Internet of Things* (IoT), which constitutes connected devices that capture information regarding movement and other sensing data of objects in the physical world, also represents a massive source of big data. IoTs can provide rich information regarding individuals' behaviors, with the resulting data being usable for increased tailoring of products, risk profiling, and pricing.

All economic transactions can be input points for digital data extraction, analysis, and assessment. This can include, therefore, every activity that is part of primary production processes, such as manufacturing, service provision, supply chain nodes, points of sale, and so on. Economic and other exchanges yield real-time data at a much deeper level than what information systems a few years old could deliver. Filtering and analyzing big data as they emerge opens the gateway to decision-making possibilities on a scale we've never witnessed in

the history of business. Within a short period of time, most enterprises turn to *cloud computing* to enable very large data sets to be stored
and processed. This is because of the level of on-demand processing
capabilities enabled that are highly scalable and cost-efficient. Storage
and processing ability have become particularly important as digital
tools such as blockchains and IoTs add to the mix of structured and
unstructured information-producing technologies.

Big data analysis offers value but also raises important challenges for organizations that accountants need to be aware of. There
exist challenges that have to do with how the data is obtained, its
processing, and its overall management and interpretation. An organization moving in the direction of big data evaluation and analysis
must contend with how it intends to deal with the onslaught of data
whose magnitude is increasing, and the types of technologies that
will enable eliciting insights from the data accessed. Naturally, speed
is of the essence so the data has to be both accessed and processed
rapidly. The data must be seen as fit for purpose and resources allocated to its validation, security, and style and receptivity by decision
makers. A first significant challenge for any enterprise has to do with
the volume, variety, speed of growth, as well as the diversity, veracity,
and visualization of the data. And then there will be the issues of
processing the data, which will entail being aware of how it is acquired
and how it is warehoused, cleansed, and mined, as well as questions
concerning data aggregation, integration, modeling, and interpretation. All this brings up a variety of technical, managerial, and ethical
issues that must be addressed.

Big data is multistructured and appropriate management mechanisms are required to enable the acquisition of different data types
from a diversity of places. Following this, data must be contextualized
so they can be analyzed to create information that is of value and ultimately convertible into knowledge for the enterprise. Data must also
be stored electronically and warehoused so it can be centrally accessed
with the help of business intelligence tools. Effective warehousing is
essential too to enable the mining of the data and its cleansing so any
corrupt elements are removed. Once this is undertaken, aggregation
and integration of the data enables summarization for statistical analysis. Modeling of the data eliminates redundancies and reorganizes the

data so it is logically and cost effectively stored. Interpretation of the data is finally possible and the information producer – which increasingly will be the accountant in the context of business and financial intelligence – should highlight aspects of the data's meaning – for instance, in terms of whether it shows causation or simple correlations (see Figure 2.3). Some of this may be qualitative aside from quantitative data reporting. Management challenges that enterprises must reflect on include dealing with privacy, security, governance, sharing of information, and ownership concerns.

Organizations engaged in big data analyses perceive huge benefits. Assessing resource availability and trends, market research, pricing options, differential product mixes, risk control elements, yield management issues, and much more can be derived from big data analyses. In theory, all this data can be granularized and personalized pretty much for any person on the planet using digital platforms and accessing every enterprise transaction and flow. Digital data can be combined to yield customer profiles and content information that enterprises have never had access to before, which can enable product offerings to be made to meet unmet needs in markets, even if those needs are not yet anticipated by consumers themselves. Already, we are used to online promotions that are tailored to our known past experiences and preferences, but digital data analyses that draw on a

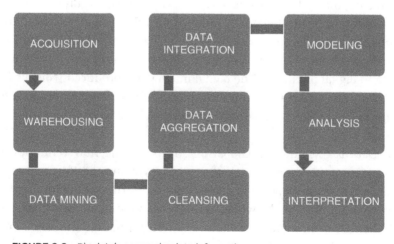

FIGURE 2.3 Big data's conversion into information.

growing mix of interacting digital applications can provide predictive insights that portend the needs of product users to a level beyond anything we've seen in the past.

The growth of data then has led to advances in modes of analysis to extract insights. Statistical approaches and qualitative and other quantitative analytical techniques that permit big data exploration are well established. These have enabled computations, transformations, and the summarizing of information. Learning algorithms allow advanced analytics with mathematical models embedded in software and sensitized to data patterns to direct us to future trends. This makes data the new oil that mobilizes not just business growth and in some cases industry-level disruptions, but also major economic shifts across nations. In data genesis, digitalization has in fact unleashed a new form of economic power.

Let's consider Nigeria as an example. Africa's largest country by population and its biggest oil producer exports crude oil, which gets refined and reimports it as expensive distilled petroleum products. Its weak refining capacity forces it to pay a high price for imported fuels. To this extent, industrial adeptness counts for something in the physical economy. The process of transforming raw material is more valuable than the raw material itself. However, the transforming process is subject to being replaced by technological advances. There is a large degree of commodification with the lowest priced processor attracting most of the business. Now take the digital economy, which is a different beast altogether. Global data value chains reward those with the capacity to take advantage of data shifts. A country like Nigeria with its large population is rapidly becoming a provider of raw data to digital platforms. The digital intelligence produced ("distilled") by platform owners in distant technology hubs, gets "reimported" into Nigeria by its source providers in the form of local data intelligence – at a solid price.

Data is the new oil. Global platforms are the new refineries of data. Strong fortunes in data processing favor stronger fortunes still. Much of the wealth accrued arises from transforming data into usable information. And all the while, entities that do more of the transforming benefit from increasing their data transformation and value creating capacity. This is because AI technologies ensure that the learning grows within the incumbent platforms. Technological advances do not offer an opening to other players. They ensure the existing player grows faster and bigger. And the agility with which data is converted by one entity into usable information does not attract the risk of becoming commoditized.

Advanced analytics can, at one level, engage AI to enable decisions without human intervention to support decision-making. The smartness of these technologies arises in that they are able to think and act like humans. We're used to Alexa and Siri, for example, that represent such types of AI applications. Increasingly we're being exposed to autonomous vehicles and robots, which are advanced types of what we've accustomed ourselves to within a very short time period. Ultimately big data analyses grow in possibilities and insights they provide. But how far enterprises should act on quantified explorations and interpretations of data is a question that finance executives will need to ask as they alter their modus operandi.

DECISION-MAKING AND INFORMATION: A WARNING!

Across enterprises, digital technologies are influencing management practices and decisions. Evidence from global surveys suggests that the most tangible benefits from big data analyses and AI systems include improved operational efficiency and cost savings, enhanced management decision-making, and better customer experience. Increased revenue, faster time to market, and more effective risk management also accrue from these. In Chapters 3, 4, and 5, we'll consider the way digitalization is impacting financial management practices and activities. For now, we look at what aspects of decision-making get altered in digitalizing environments and what must be borne in mind before executives jump on a bandwagon of changes that rest on presumptions about the role of information in decision-making and management rationales.

Information helps resolve uncertainty. It can ensure survival if not growth. Much of managerial savvy today rests on the general presumption that the best decisions have to be evidence based; that unless there is hard data analysis of formal information, decision-making will suffer. There is certainly truth that as information emerges, it should influence decisions being made, and if need be, change decisions that have been made. It has been held that when accused of changing his position, John Keynes famously noted, "When my information changes, I alter my conclusions. What do you do, sir?" Changing one's mind is a strength rather than a failure of analysis. And information should provide the reasoning for this as it should help make up as well as change one's mind. Humility and admission that one cannot assess all data as it emerges is also good to know for corporates in the information economy we inhabit. One has to learn how much to rely on information sources and how much is needed to make good decisions. This is not an easy task.

Envisioning what long-term direction an organization should steer toward is a requirement for leaders so they can rudder it along a thought-out and defined path. Shorter impact decisions can then fit into the broad directions being pursued. What must be understood, however, is that formal information analyses, objective assessments of data systems' output, and rational evaluations of quantified data are not what always underpin good corporate decisions and executive actions. The notion that "you cannot manage what you cannot measure" has gained much allure in management speak and training but rarely captures what great leaders actually do in maneuvering their enterprise on a path of progress. Intuition, wisdom, inspiration, and gut feel, have always led to many sound actions by corporate leaders.

Often, managers are indoctrinated to think that it is not commendable to justify decisions on the basis of a soft subjective sense about the right thing to do. Pressure exists for signaling to others that a structured and quantified rationale underlies decisions taken. Calculations tend to be made transparent, visible, and verifiable. Objective analyses are to be properly made and factored into major decisions and actions should be validated and undertaken only after people have cogitated in a way that lends confidence and justification for the actions taken.

In truth, good decisions often rely, at least at some level, on a feeling that the actions taken are the right ones. At times, when it seems essential to convince others, subjective inspiration is veneered with objective calculations and structured logic to get the decision collectively supported. Observing organizational decision-making and action in almost any enterprise will confirm that analytical rigor tends to also be complemented and sometimes superseded by subjective evaluations that are hidden from expression. At times, the subjectivity of decisions is muted to provide a semblance that there is objective and rational validity in the decision-making process. Technical analysis often gets privileged over subjective assessments by trained managers. Even where a decision outcome turns out to be sound, its subjective basis is usually kept silent! What must be understood is that effective decisions can derive from inspiration, gut feelings, and emotional savvy that need not be quantified and mathematized. We must see information examination in the context of its usefulness. For an organization to be data-centric is desirable, but never at the price of thinking that only formal data analysis matters.

As digitalization objectives evolve in enterprises, the finance team must learn that too much weight can be placed by individuals on trying to make management a pure science. But leaders know that management is as much an art. Much of consulting-speak and business school–derived popular writings about effective management neglect the positive role of subjective and even non-discursive decision-making inputs. This is a mistake! As the growing deluge of information takes hold across business environments, it's easy to think that everything that goes into decision-making should be quantified, but the value of soft interpretation when businesses go digital will grow rather than diminish. Where decisions have to be made more and more rapidly, they can rightly be advanced based on formalized data and empirical data that echo transactions, processes, and activities. But this should not be to the exclusion of everything that is qualitative and subjective. At another level, data that can be formalized and codified and be part of enterprise information systems supplemented with objective inscriptions such as memos, reports, financial statements, and so on, should be available in forms that can readily be exhibited quantitatively and graphically. However, knowledge is not all explicit – it is also to a degree implicit and tacit. It can be deeply grounded in the human psyche through experience, prior experimentation, personal wisdom, and context-defined insights. Such knowledge should not be crowded out by formalized information inputs into decision-making.

In the emerging digital enterprise environment, there is a growing base of information that is situation specific, dynamically emergent, not always easy to document, and that involves human interpretation. It would consequently be a mistake to tilt organizations toward solely relying on explicit knowledge about overt exchanges to drive decisions. Simply put – just because digital data is easy to codify, exists in high volume, and can be made to appear technical and objective, doesn't mean data should monopolize the basis for enterprise decisions. Finance leaders must develop an awareness of where formal analysis should be complemented with softer decision-making inputs. Given the warning about not presuming that everything that matters in management must be calculable and formally data driven, we can now discuss why the digital era also needs to have managers dispense with concepts they take to be second nature. We do this in Chapter 3.

NOTES

1. Kitone. 2019. *11 Digital Transformation Quotes To Lead Change & Inspire Action*. *Medium* (May 6). https://medium.com/digital-transformation-talk/11-digital-transformation-quotes-to-lead-change-inspire-action-a81a3aa79a45

2. Edwards, N. 2020. The digital side of Deutsche Bank that you have not heard about. *Forbes* (February 24). https://www.forbes.com/sites/neiledwards/2020/02/24/the-digital-side-of-deutsche-bank-that-you-have-not-heard-about/#78fd971f1ade

3. AAA. Committee to Prepare a Statement of Basic Accounting Theory. 1966. *A Statement of Basic Accounting Theory*. Evanston, IL: AAA.

4. Williams, T. 2020. How digital transformation enables modern accounting. *Blackline Magazine* (October 8). https://www.blackline.com/blog/finance-performance-management/digital-transformation-enables-modern-accounting/

5. Fagella, D. 2020. *AI in the Accounting Big Four – Comparing Deloitte, PwC, KPMG, and EY*. *Emerj* (April 3). https://emerj.com/ai-sector-overviews/ai-in-the-accounting-big-four-comparing-deloitte-pwc-kpmg-and-ey/

6. Jiang, L. 2019.The last mile problem: Understanding the economics affecting the future of blockchain. *Data Driven Investor* (April 26). https://www.datadriveninvestor.com/2019/04/26/the-last-mile-problem-understanding-the-economics-affecting-the-future-of-blockchain/#

7. Bradley, R. 2020. *Blockchain explained . . . in under 100 words*. Deloitte. https://www2.deloitte.com/ch/en/pages/strategy-operations/articles/blockchain-explained.html

8. Deloitte Insights. 2019. *Deloitte's 2019 Global Blockchain Survey*. https://www2.deloitte.com/content/dam/Deloitte/se/Documents/risk/DI_2019-global-blockchain-survey.pdf

9. Price, D. 2020. 5 blockchain problems: Security, privacy, legal, regulatory, and ethical issues. *Blocks Decoded* (March 23). https://blocksdecoded.com/blockchain-issues-security-privacy-legal-regulatory-ethical/

10. Grewal-Carr, V., and Marshall, S., eds. 2016. *Blockchain. Enigma. Paradox. Opportunity*. Deloitte. https://www2.deloitte.com/content/dam/Deloitte/uk/Documents/Innovation/deloitte-uk-blockchain-full-report.pdf

11. Guinard, D., and Ogee, A. 2019. Blockchain is not a magic bullet for security. Can it be trusted? World Economic Forum (August 19). https://www.weforum.org/agenda/2019/08/blockchain-security-trust/

12. Ray, S., Villa, A., Tornhohm, C., Rashid, N., and Alexander, M. 2020. Gartner magic quadrant for robotic process automation. Gartner (July 27). https://www.gartner.com/en/documents/3988021

CHAPTER **3**

The Trouble
with Finance

New business models continue to emerge as technology disrupts how, when, and where business is done. Our value ... moves from "expertise" to one of "agility" and continuous reinvention.[1]

—Andrew Harding, chief executive
of Management Accounting for the Association of
International Certified Professional Accountants

"Here's how donations work. You roll up your sleeve. A blood donation service takes the blood. They ship it under strict temperature requirements to a production site. They separate it into other products. And they take it to a hospital or blood bank. But then they lose visibility," says Warren Tomlin (digital and innovation leader for EY Canada).[2] Canadian Blood Services wanted a better approach to get near real-time visibility and traceability of blood products throughout the blood's journey. EY applied a blockchain solution to this: when a donation occurs, the unit is scanned and all the related blood data is put on the blockchain. As the products from that donation move through the supply network, they are scanned repeatedly with their location and status recorded on a single, unified platform. Tomlin says: "Every time we get an Internet of Things (IoT) update of the temperature, it's recorded on the blockchain. Every time we know where it is by GPS, that's recorded on the blockchain. If you think about blockchain and that chain of custody, we end up creating an improved audit trail for these products. A single visible one that stretches from donor to recipient." As the system develops, Canadian Blood Services will install artificial intelligence and machine learning platforms to analyze that data with increasing depth of detail.

Management has evolved paradigms since the 1950s that we have simply stopped questioning. These must be unlearned. There is nothing fundamentally permanent about business fundamentals! Conventional folklore as to what is rational in business is ultimately received opinion about what works well for a time, but revisiting such opinion is essential. We'll see in this chapter that old business rationales face severe limits in the digital era and that what is conventionally accepted about managing enterprises is becoming obsolete. The trouble with finance is that many defunct paradigms guide the work and advice that finance teams provide. Some reassessing is necessary.

Pretty much all commercial enterprises today need to consider the market for their products or services and the resources required to operate. Assessments of the competition, supply chain involvement, and factors such as product substitutes and other risks and challenges in delivering value have to be looked at. Treasury conditions also need to be evaluated and monitored via business plans and budgets, and financing requirements from investors and lenders must be worked out. But with digital, what is different is that we no longer live in a world of linear logic. Our assumptions need changing. We explore this here.

BUSINESS IS NO LONGER LINEAR

Digitalization can drive an enterprise toward models of operations that disrupt conventional notions of step-by-step processes and sequential production, sales, delivery, service, and supply chain paths. Unlike traditional businesses, digitalized companies operate within *continuous feedback loops* where their control functions and decisions are integrated. They replace dated planning and control pathways with ongoing experimentation and assessments of market, product, competition, and environmental changes. Data cannot be constrained in form, structure, or type, or this will give an incomplete picture of what matters and the nature of signals necessary to pivot the business when needed. Information that is relevant should be able to point to the need for minor alterations or total revisions of the business hypothesis currently driving a company's actions. Signals should be able to point to broad redirection of objectives or toward activities that need reconfiguration or simply to fine-tune processes to better address user requirements. In many ways, the shape and content conventional financial reporting takes requires extensive revisions and rethinking because accounting presumes that resources and transactions are linear. But the digital world is interactive, multifaceted, and increasingly networked such that data will obey new laws that are more complex and diverse.

The flow of data in digital is one thing. But time is now especially of the essence. With more and more signals mounting, responsive action must be effected very quickly. A consequence of this is that the financing implications of actions taken in digitalized firms need to circumvent the usual manner in which finance gets approved and released. RPA and AI systems enable digitally transforming enterprises to see market changes and product evolutions in new ways. As a result, old models for planning and controlling where preset targets and actual outcomes are compared before the next set of actions can be taken no longer work. In fact, it's likely there is little to compare new experiences with. Plans and budgets cannot continue to be effective preludes to what may happen later. We need to move much beyond calls for "beyond budgeting." The here and now becomes more relevant in digital so dated planning and control perspectives need to be shed. The sequential and linear logic finance executives have been trained to expect (see Figure 3.1) as part of enterprise decision-making no longer exists. Sound and rational business logic used to imply that data from transactions should be converted into useful information for executives to analyze and decide on what actions to put into effect after which outcomes can be compared vis-a-vis what was anticipated. This has changed.

Of significance is that in digitalized environments, the sequential flow from data to action may be shortened where data analysis and action become integrated via RPA systems. AI systems enable data sources that continuously grow in their structured and unstructured forms to feed into action outcomes (see Figure 3.2). Little room exists here for action tied to conventional logics relating to data flows.

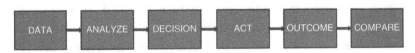

Figure 3.1 Linearity in traditional business.

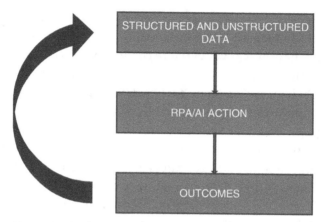

Figure 3.2 Digitalized data and organizational action.

Decision-making by humans must rest on altered financial management mechanisms where new digital technologies operate along altered parameters. The connections between customers, consumers, and products, and services do not conform to norms of Industrial Age business wisdom. Market creation, size, location, and production issues require a whole new basis for financial configuration as costs and financial flows accord to different principles, and the business no longer lives entirely within linear sequences of organizational functions and transactions. Aside from the sequential flow of resources in business around which accounting reports are produced, what has become evident over the recent decades is that qualitative information is as relevant as quantitative. But in an automated technology-intense environment, it is wise for organizations to not ignore the role of tacit and subjective input into decisions. We briefly made this point in the previous chapter and more will be said about this later, as in firms shifting to digital, what must prevail are decisions that couple both automated and human information elements. Soft information can be highly valuable and justified in influencing actions taken.

STRATEGY FOLKLORE

Linear flows also have changed how firms strategize. Let's look at what we know about strategy and see what digital does to this.[3] Michael

Porter – widely regarded as the godfather of corporate strategy – has extensively influenced business thought over the past 40 years. He has shaped how executives visualize competitive forces and corporate strategies. He posits three generic strategies for firms seeking to make abnormally high profits. Some adopt a *differentiation* approach gaining market share with unique products that customers place high value on and pay a premium for. Other firms seek to be *cost leaders*, stressing cost cutting to offer lower prices to large numbers of customers. Certain firms also use a *focus* strategy that exhibits cost leadership or differentiation within niche markets. For differentiators, the finance function homes in on accounting tools such as quality function deployment, strategic cost analysis, and differential pricing in managing differentiated products. Accounting techniques favored by cost leaders include standard costing and variance analysis, activity-based costing, and structured budgetary controls over the life cycle of products. A company that falls somewhere between being a differentiator and a cost leader yields, at best, average profitability but will likely lose its market. Porter suggests that to get things right, five competitive forces must be heeded no matter what: the number and capabilities of competitors; the ability of customers to find a substitute product; the ease with which suppliers can raise prices; the ease with which customers can lower prices; and the potential threat posed by competitors. Moreover, it is purported that investment evaluation techniques should take account of the strategic orientation of a business.

How relevant are Porter's views in digitalizing enterprises? Digital platforms are about interconnections and integrating aspects of value chains as much as possible. In digital settings, the five forces need not always be balanced to earn a company the most power. Bypassing the five forces can point firms to value creation possibilities through disruptive business models. It would not make sense for instance if Amazon stopped giving customers the option of buying from third-party sellers given that such sales earn Amazon commissions and data from the commercial activities of these sellers. Greater value can be given to customers through lower pricing, as well as enhance the company's profitability. It may be better to seek to extend current limits, and through interconnections and the integration of single value chains, to create value.

The five forces make assumptions about required investments and focus on working smarter within bounded parameters of business structures. But working smarter in a digital business implies moving beyond those boundaries. Airbnb's impact on travel accommodation comes not from a model of investing in premium properties or commoditized cheaper dwellings. Its philosophy rests on pushing transaction costs right down and taking a very small cut on a high volume of activity across property types. Just competing with hotels would mean a business model based on the acquisition of real estate. Instead, Airbnb uses digital technology that brings together existing capacity such that its cut is very low, but high volume drives profits. The resulting supply unleashed onto the market lowers prices for clients who share in the value creation. The value Airbnb manages to create arises from the savings that consumers make on costs redistributed away from hotels, going back to customers and of course to Airbnb itself. Uber's approach is similar to Airbnb's. Its technology enhances flexibility for users and drivers with value being distributed away from traditional taxi and transportation providers. Value goes to drivers using their own vehicles, who with Uber's technological support offer alternative travel options to customers. Because value is passed on to customers in both these companies, their receptiveness to the service is enhanced and the overall market grows. The upshot is a positive net effect going beyond simply substituting one kind of service for another. The five forces perspective and its decision-making rationale would have curtailed the worldview required to think through the type of disruption we're witnessing in the accommodation or transportation markets.

In relation to investment approvals, the finance function usually applies capital budgeting litmus tests and finance tends to rule the roost in corporate life. But in many enterprises its processes are inadequate and at times even antiquated. For instance for a particular project to be given the green light, the proposal needs to identify cash flow projections at predefined time nodes so that actual versus planned outcomes can be monitored and anticipated investment returns tracked. Imposing this dated discipline as if digitalization initiatives can accord with Industrial Age accounting mechanics is unworkable. ITC people will readily recognize that a different frame of reference is required when considering digital investments. Digital transformation projects that bring increased flexibility, enterprise agility, and greater responsiveness to market changes and competitor ploys do not tie in with conventional investment structures where cash-flow forecasts can be time demarcated.

Digitalization is about dealing with uncertainty, speed, and the continuous mobilizing of rapid maneuvers. Accordingly, projects need to be implemented following fast iterative assessments by different functions within the enterprise that do not conform to the strictures of traditional financial controls. Digital initiatives tend to spread out and impact areas that may not even have been envisaged at the initial outlay assessment stage. It's essential to evaluate proposals within a wider comprehension of what is really at play beyond the narrow confines which have served finance for decades. Working out accurate returns on investments, project residual incomes, or net present values is not difficult; but questions must be asked whether such metrics fit into the realm of dynamic value creation on a day-to-day basis from digital transformations. Trying to quantify projects within the parameters of bureaucratized accounting with the application of conventional appraisal techniques and narrow conceptions of value creation and operations is no longer viable.

What's more, digital initiatives regarded by finance as capital projects often transition into operational expenses. For instance, software-on-demand or cloud-based services can replace in-house systems but they can also be much more than this. While accounting professionals understand risk-return trade-offs, they may not display the entrepreneurial base that undergirds digitalization projects. Returns may result from a small subset of projects that can be captured within detailed accounting analyses, but the real payoff overlooked by accounting may well be the extensive agility acquired that helps fend off competitors and ensures the firm remains ahead of the pack. Financial mechanisms that worked in the past may go unquestioned, but they'll miss the implicit essence of digital transformation projects. Building tomorrow requires more than living by yesterday's precepts about the probability, magnitude, and timing of cash flows that investments in digital present.

Naturally, all firms still have to think about the competition, suppliers, customers, and so on. These are generic market forces. But what is key is to recognize that in the new digitally advanced world, value creation takes place along different structures and under different principles with different systems of interactions that are continuing to evolve and which defy traditional routes and sequencing of organizational growth. The application of accounting tools such as activity-based costing, standard costing and variance analysis, tight budgetary controls analysis, and product life cycle costing as well as capital investment appraisal techniques all need to be rethought in digital. If Porter is still to be drawn on, then it's to the extent that digitalization not just enables but makes essential cost leadership objectives to be pursued while concurrently delivering on differentiation goals (Figure 3.3) and taking advantage of the enhanced agility digital technologies tender. This is a whole new ballgame.

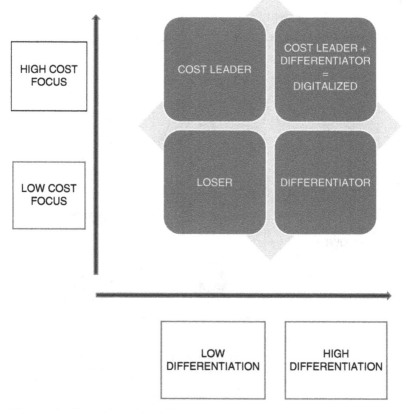

Figure 3.3 Strategy is no longer binary.

THE IMPORTANCE OF "?s"

Over 50 years ago, the Boston Consulting Group's Bruce Henderson proposed the concept of the *growth share matrix*. The matrix identifies market growth and market share as two dimensions that affect a firm's products (or business units) to help us work out how to address opportunities in the face of limited resources. Figure 3.4 identifies the products in the matrix quadrants – cash cows, dogs, question marks, and stars – and their desirability.

The dimensions of the matrix shown in Figure 3.4 are ensconced in business parlance and regularly referred to in marketing, strategy, and finance communications. The matrix bears significant implications for accounting mechanisms used to control and manage these different product types from pricing to costing to investment and cash budgeting concerns. It suggests that real cash-producing products are the "cash cows" shown within the high market share/low growth quadrant. These cows can generate much cash because, in part, their high

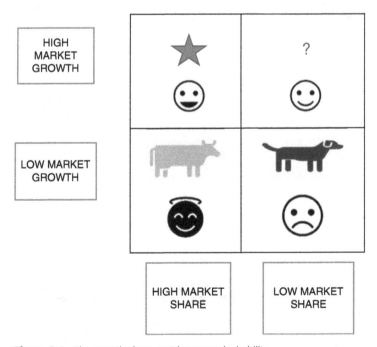

Figure 3.4 The growth share matrix versus desirability.

market share wards off new competitors who would find it difficult to gain traction against big-market players with process knowledge, efficiencies, and brand recognition. In addition, with market growth slowing, new competitors will probably not want to invest, opting instead for other emerging opportunities. To market incumbents, these products enjoy relatively high revenues, high customer retention, and low costs. The problem is that as the market matures, the products will be replaced by new alternatives and customer needs may themselves have evolved.

Aside from cash cows, dogs may be part of a firm's product portfolio. These animals operate in the low market share/low growth quadrant and do not produce cash. They could be products with negative profitability that should be gotten rid of unless there is a way to rethink their value or rebrand them.

The future is always a question mark. A "?" product could be highly innovative, operating in a space exhibiting market growth. Naturally, by their nature, question-mark products need large investments in attempts to gain market share and ultimately to possibly yield high returns. Finance executives know that decisions about whether a question-mark product is worth supporting will require much analysis. Such a product needs cash resources, and there is a high risk that it may never attain profitability. However, they are essential to ensuring a company's longer-term survival.

A successful "?" that increases its share in an expanding market will become a "star" product. Executives tend to favor star products that exist in the high market share/high growth corner. These will require some continued investment in advertising, promotion, and upgrading so as to retain and/or increase market traction. Stars can face aggressive competition from other companies jockeying for a position in this space, but it is important they counter this, as a larger share in a growing market will potentially deliver very high returns.

For the finance function, the growth share matrix is useful because where there are multiple products, much thought must be given on how to allocate scarce resources and the accounting tools to use as products change quadrants. The way enterprises have tended to visualize the life cycle of a product is that once the product is launched, if the market for the product grows, competition will intensify. Weaker businesses will drop out of the market and sales revenues for incumbents staying the course will grow until a maturity plateau is reached. Only a few major players will remain, each with high market share. When demand for the product starts to drop off, the product will go into decline, reaching dog status. A "?" product that is supported and in demand will gain market share and become a star. After some intense competition, only a few stars will arise and over time cash cows will emerge. Before or when the product reaches the end of its maturity phase, an innovation will displace the older product. Cash cows then are rationalized as being highly valued in producing a source of earning, which can then be channeled into sponsoring question marks' growth trajectories and sustaining emerging stars. This is because few competitors will enter a space where large operators hold higher shares in markets witnessing diminishing growth. Moreover, cash cows will have fathomed ways of producing efficiently and learned how to achieve customer satisfaction and loyalty. Where prices can be maintained and costs minimized, large market penetration will yield large returns.

How relevant is the product matrix conceptualization when a firm is digital? Stars are product concepts that already have a high share of a high growth market. They can require further cash input to keep growing fast and scale up in competitive markets. In a sense, star status instead of cash cow status should be the end game in digital business environments because continuous innovation, market expansion, and growth of market share underpin what stars aim for. Low market growth, regardless of share, cannot be what an enterprise would target because it will be too short-lived. Moreover, digital can imply high fixed cost and low variable cost structures, which galvanize the pursuit of market expansion to yield high contributions past the break-even point. Further, maturity phases in product lives within digitalized enterprises may be very narrow if they exist at all, depending on the firm's products. Homing in on cash cows is not what digital can be about.

Novel products that are digital themselves or produced by firms that are digitally transformed can belong in the matrix's dog category. The product may be so innovative that it resides in the low market share/low growth space being a little ahead of its time. The product could show incredible promise for both market growth as well as share in the future. In digital, it should not be a kneejerk reaction that dogs are what dogs are in traditional industrial companies, where they are viewed typically as deadweight and readily dispensable, other than for very specific strategic reasons. It may make more sense to invest resources into backing a dog in digital spaces, especially if there are signs that demand for the products can be triggered through market education of customers who only need to experiment with the product before becoming hooked.

Virgin Galactic evidently had no market share or growth when it invested in developing spacecrafts in 2004. It is now close to completing Federal Aviation Administration milestones with the requisite number of successful rocket-powered test flights. After this, it will be at a stage where its market is predicted to grow to at least 100 to 200 people boarding its ships annually and potentially generating $50 to $100 million average annual revenues in addition to tourist flights. The company currently has over 600 passengers who have paid between $200,000 to $250,000 each for a ticket, and hundreds more are placing their deposits. Such extremely entrepreneurial projects born in the Industrial Age can become a normal part of business in digitally transformed firms. Of necessity is the deployment of data to supercharge executive insights on the potential worth of lower-right-quadrant initiatives.

Digital enterprises may see dogs with low market growth and share in terms of the growth capacity they can achieve in a market they themselves create. Transcending conventional ideas about what is viable and doable has to be rethought. Data analysis enables that. In digital, a product should ideally not become a cash cow, because high market share could trigger further market growth through understanding changing products and customer needs, as well as competitor advances. The star will be the goal where high market share and continued growth of the market are enjoyed (see Figure 3.5). Income should increase as maturity phases get extended with refinements to the product. Profits that translate into cash flows can be used to finance continued business activities. Again, in a digital context the growth matrix takes a different meaning and requires alternative

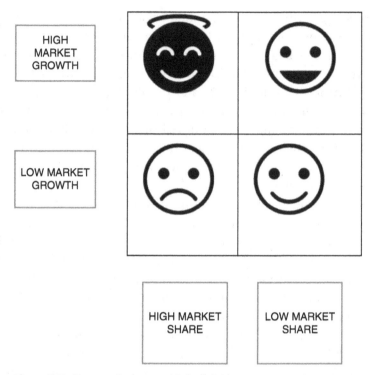

Figure 3.5 The growth share matrix in digital.

rationales underlying decisions to manage profitability. The finance function has to learn to provide the right type of information for effective decisions that often do not and should not echo conventional Industrial Age thinking.

HIGH SALES VOLUME MEANS HIGH PROFITS, RIGHT?

Few would contest that a company making more rather than less profit on every product sold and selling more of these products rather than less will enlarge its overall profit. So, any business should make sure its products contribute as much as possible to profit, and that they achieve the highest possible volume of sales. In Figure 3.6, it's the top right quadrant, A, you want to be in – with a high volume of sales, as well as high contribution from each sale. B products are profitable at the unit level, but you need to sell more of them to get higher profits. C products

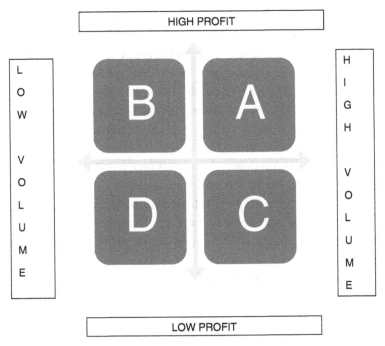

Figure 3.6 Unit profit versus consumer volume.

give low profit per unit, or even make a loss, so could be the most problematic. They need to move up the profit contribution line. D products might also be making a loss, but are only selling in low numbers.

In digitalized businesses, one has to look deeper to see how far the cardinal accounting rule of higher profit/higher volume applies. We'll need to consider who actually uses the firm's output. Do they pay directly for this, or are there paying customers who are attracted to these consumers? Using Google to search online does not require a payment for this service, but advertisers are Google's customers who pay for access to search engine users. Does Google's consumer of search output get a better service if more people search? Yes – because Google learns from each search carried out and enhances search result quality for subsequent users. Search services continually improve and more users get attracted to use the search engine. Bettering the service incurs costs, but advertisers get attracted by the growing user base and Google's revenues rise as a result.

It's the same for Newsmax. It has users who consume what the platform publishes, but the actual customers are the advertisers and companies that purchase user data and eyeballs. Google wants users to make a high volume of searches, with the product costing Google quite a bit before it can be delivered to the customer (the advertisers). Newsmax likewise has the task of delivering the right kinds of users to ads, and the right data to paying customers. This, despite the fact that, like all commercial businesses, they ultimately want a large base of customers who buy products, and to get high profits on these. What are the products? To a certain extent, the user is the product since users represent the potential of impressions on visitors that advertisers seek and pay for.

If we think of our product profitability boxes in terms of customers, then we might say advertisers move from B to A – as users increase in Figure 3.6. They might have been at level C or perhaps D if the revenues they generated fell below the cost to service the advertisements. If we consider users in terms of the profitability boxes, then Google and Newsmax have quadrant C as their objective, rather than A. Customers, of course, should ideally be at A.

Juxtaposing users and customers suggests something quite rare in the industrial world. The services provided by the platform are not the products that generate revenues. To a degree the product is the search engine user or Newsmax reader. Yet the users get a product that to them delivers value in the form of a service. In accounting terms, there is dissociation between the top revenue line and the expenses line items that relate to search service provision. Growth in these expenses powers growth in the revenues rather than the other way around. Accounting convention presumes that sales growth implies expenses growth, and the margin is what must be monitored to up profit alongside volume. The accountant's focus then will be on providing costing information on the product to feed into decisions about pricing and revenue growth strategies. In fact, in digital, cost containment remains all important, but expense increases can spell upcoming revenue growth! Times are changing!

HOW DO NEW TECHNOLOGIES DISRUPT ACCOUNTING?

With digital, how should finance executives conceptualize the information required to enhance a firm's decisions so it manages more effectively and grows its bottom line? There are different facets of this. First, one must understand that digitalization implies an altered value creation model. An enterprise must seek to use technologies to create value both for users and customers (where these are different). The value to users must be delivered while generating value for the firm through better servicing of customers. The new relationship between revenues and expenses in digital is a key point for finance executives to grasp because *a new divide may exist between customers and users*. In other words in Figure 3.6, "A" type customers must see returns in dealing with the enterprise that exceed their costs of dealing with the firm and they must perceive value to have been created for them. In assessing this, the enterprise will itself realize value because the user base driving most of the expenses also will find and create value that helps mobilize greater customer attraction. Accounting's disruption implies a deeper managerial information provider role for finance professionals who need to understand, detect, and communicate new opportunities opened up by business going digital.

Digital alters traditional value creation models so much that new lines get drawn, and these make consumers distinct from customers. If your service users are the product, and your customers pay for that product, then financial management information will have to be different. What's clear is that the volume of users matters hugely, and profit per customer only has a very indirect relationship to consumer volume. The finance executive needs to extract information that moves away from accounting metrics and ratios that were useful old-world parameters of effective business management but are no longer so.

Second, the new parameters of business entail a network of relationships rather than linear and sequential logic of where value lies. Let's explore this further. Most industrial firms traditionally use two key accounting levers to drive profits. They try to maximize volume of sales, which will consequently intensify production volumes. As volume grows, so costs can be worked on to judiciously bring them down perhaps by capturing scale economies until an inflection point is reached where further expansion of production capacity has to be invested into. Such firms, will strategically recognize that investments in scope must also be made. Product type expansions will increase a firm's scope of production, which potentially attracts more customers and opens up new sales channels. As scope grows, interrelationships between products and operational processes also arise and create joint costs incurred in delivering a multiplicity of products. Scope-of-product increases reflect marketing savvy where customers and users get greater product choice as a requisite for business growth. This means more sharing of common resources at the product unit level as well as at the batch level of production and often also at the broader facility level.

These commercial strategies pointed toward harnessing scale and scope advantages particularly from the 1970s on. This, at the time, led to demands on accountants to provide more accurate information on individual products, customers, and strategies. Cost management techniques such as throughput accounting, target costing, functional analysis, and activity-based costing and activity-based management were born out of these business trends during the last decades of the twentieth century. They were accounting solutions meant mainly for linear and sequential production contexts. For many organizations these accounting techniques continue to prove useful. Digital has, however, created new possibilities that these tools, at best, are only partially equipped to address. Digitalized enterprises are highly networked and their *values chains have numerous crossovers*. What's more, users of digital products and digital products themselves have partly, through IoT technologies, become key players in product design. Users emit noneconomic data as do products. Understanding that enterprises are part of networks that they themselves propagate rather than inhabiting linear production chains of goods and services for sale, and recognizing that the networks they create present possibilities for deriving market information, is essential to fully extract the gems digitalization offers. Organizations that have the wherewithal to recognize and leverage such a view of data analysis will win, hands down, over ones that do not.

Third, though decision-making information provided by the finance function is principally aimed at humans, there must be cognizance that humans do not have a monopoly on learning! The concept of learning organizations has been on executives' minds for a long time. But digital takes this to a whole new level. Learning must occur as data and information arrive, rather than just before or after, and finance executives do not have to assume that their output only has to do with individuals via whom decisions get made.

Some services and products become better as their usage grows. For instance, search engine results get better as users make more use of the engine because the service provider is able to better the product through learning from consumers. Likewise, decisions should exhibit quality improvements as the volume of information analyzed grows. The finance executive's role in the organization must become one where data sources translate into decisions that are fruitful, whatever form the agent takes. And finance should seek to algorithmically ground decision-making into machine agents where appropriate. Digital transformation must ultimately be about an enterprise becoming so data-centric that where decisions can be made virtually through automation, they should be. The data appealed to should grow such that they lead to more effective decisions, which then generate better and more expansive data pools for further deployment. Data's consequences should be more data and more machine grounded decisions, because with data volume growth comes learning. This creates *continuous positive loops of improvements* that become difficult for a competitor to break through.

A fourth point that finance executives should heed is that while connections between products matter, the number of connections between users can also grow and become part of the product proposition. Products may engender value from interconnections. Members of TripAdvisor, for example, get greater value as the base of TripAdvisor users grows. A little content attracts consumers, who then start to contribute to the content. This then attracts more users. So, consumers become producers of content, which fuels further user engagement. The greater the value to each user, the more the network grows in size. Network effects can enable fast growth in user base by offering implicit value growth. Alibaba attracts users (buyers) if it has more users (sellers), and sellers are also attracted as the number of buyers goes up. Indeed.com attracts job-seekers because of the number of job advertisers, and that numbers goes up as the volume of job-seekers grows. Similarly so with LinkedIn. Google's searches, as we suggested, grow in quality as more users carry out searches, because information from past searches is fed back into algorithms that have "learned" to enhance the value of output. As with our earlier point, user numbers matter a great deal because the more users there are, the more they'll flock to the service provider. As they do, more data trails get created, which assists in determining evolving trends and insights that feed into decisions.

A threshold volume of a product's users may have to be reached, which then triggers more volume growth. When the scale of that volume picks up, it can generate extreme value growth. When a company provides a service to users, costs increase on a one-to-one basis. That is to say, the company incurs costs at the same rate as the number of users grows. But, past a certain point where users get value out of other users joining the platform, value just grows at an accelerated pace. Accounting insight is essential to pick up these *inflection points*. Where network effects are at play, costs will only grow linearly while value will expand exponentially. It is the finance executive's responsibility to be sensitized to plausible data inputs from network effects or information that can direct the enterprise toward harnessing network effects more effectively.

WHAT NOW?

We've seen that Porter's framing of strategic issues does not fully tally with business going digital. Past strategies can be countered with new technologies, which allow us to redistribute and/or create value. Rather than using a pure "five forces" focus, tech firms have altered the dynamics of competition. They can completely bypass the hurdles that were there in the industrial economy meaning we need to rethink better business strategies for digitalized firms. This could imply using technologies to combine mass customization, innovation, and premium offerings, such as to exhibit both cost leadership and differentiation. We may need to ponder whether high volume within a market must be concomitant with high profits from sales. Further, we've seen that, for digitalized enterprises, thinking about the difference between customers and consumers is important. Customers generate revenues, and consumers generate costs. This breaks the links between the two in a way that finance teams are not used to. The cart can now come before the horse: expense increases can portend revenue rises. So this means we need to think differently about profit per sale and consumer growth. On top of that, some digital firms enjoy network effects. Because value can grow exponentially, while costs show only linear growth, this gives a totally different angle on how firms might manage resources and grow revenues, costs, and income. Immediate maximization of profits may not be the best approach because of these wider effects. Taken together, these characteristics point to growth in user volume and value creation taking shape in a manner considerably different in digital environments. We dig into this a little deeper in Chapter 4.

NOTES

1. *The new paradigm: Andrew Harding, FCMA, CGMA.* 2018. https://www
.fm-magazine.com/issues/2018/aug/new-paradigm-andrew-harding.html

2. Tomlin, W. 2020. *How blockchain is helping make every blood donation more effective.* EY. https://www.ey.com/en_gl/better-begins-with-you/how-block chain-could-ensure-every-drop-of-blood-is-tracked-and-every-outcome-is-measured

3. Porter, M. 1979. How competitive forces shape strategy. *Harvard Business Review* (March). https://hbr.org/1979/03/how-competitive-forces-shape-strategy Porter, M. 1980. *Competitive Strategy: Techniques for Analyzing Industries and Competitors.* New York: Free Press; and Porter, M. 1985. *The Competitive Advantage: Creating and Sustaining Superior Performance.* New York: Free Press.

CHAPTER **4**

As If Managing Costs Mattered

We're going to go digital. We want to be able to get to a place where you can raise a work order, order a part, get it delivered, install it, be invoiced, [and] pay for it. We want that chain to be touchless. If we can do that it will take out 30% to 40% of our cost.[1]

—Bernard Looney, CEO, BP

It's been almost 20 years since we've seen the average price of crude oil drop below $30 a barrel.[2] Today, every oil company is trying to reduce operating and labor costs to survive. Many large unconventional oil reserves in the United States have been tapped into, which has lowered prices as supply has risen. But that's only part of the story. Automation technologies, cloud computing, and advanced analytics are making oil producers gain competitiveness. Equinor forecasts a $3 billion improvement in free cash flow from digital by 2025 to be driven by its CEO Anders Opedal's passion for "technology and digitalization."[3] AI-centered software at Shell and BP's digitalization efforts are also expected to deliver benefits in the billions of dollars. What's digital got to do with oil? Digitalization enables the collection and analysis of data from pumps on oil rigs and compressors in refineries as well as headsets worn by field workers. Aggregating this data statistically and deploying AI tools enables oil companies to monitor and control oil field machinery remotely and optimize energy use. The costs of labor, energy, machine maintenance, and back-office operations fall, and the amount of oil a company produces rises. At a time when oil companies are reducing capital investments, digitalization picks up the slack, helping predict when machine parts will fail. And as the workforce in oil and gas shrinks, remote monitoring and automation technologies allow operations with fewer people, with algorithms doing the work of certain technicians or supervisors. In fact, digitalization can cut the cost of refining a barrel of oil by over 10% – a crucial amount when the world is experiencing hard times.[4]

You need more than technology to extract value from technology. Going digital isn't enough – it needs to be commercially operational-ized, or failure will ensue. We've seen business principles lagging tech-nology before. In the 1980s, enterprises needed to react to a growth of competition from firms that were deploying new technologies enabling them to deliver products and services faster, at lower cost, with greater variety and yielding more value for the customer. Businesses that invested more into these flexible and more advanced technologies of the time found that appropriate operational outcomes could not be had without more useful accounting information. Accounting's focus on aggregate reporting earnings benefitted investors and external parties but not decision makers who needed to take product related and pro-cess specific actions. They could not do so in the dark. Accounting information failed to reflect technological advances and firms lost out making incorrect decisions based on financial systems that were out-dated. Finance leaders, business school professors, consultants, and accounting thinkers eventually came up with novel accounting tools for executives to make business decisions more aligned with the tech-nological innovations that were implemented. What novel accounting tools emerged to help firms extract the benefits of new technologies? Techniques such as throughput and activity accounting, quality cost-ing, target cost management, and balanced scorecards gained popu-larity as managers recognized their value in enhancing their decisions. Cost management and pricing decisions could be better thought through and assessing competitor and essential market changes was made more workable through these new accounting applications.

Today, technological change is similarly much ahead of finance. Accounting disruption stands at our doorstep and realignment is once again needed urgently. The field cannot await displacement by other information solutions that do not have the accounting wherewithal and firepower that finance based managerial tools are capable of delivering. We look in this chapter at how certain basic concepts which have long guided financial information for internal decision makers need reconsideration. An element of current accounting should remain in place for many com-panies though those practices that need re-tuning will need to be acted upon fast. Accounting's disruption will stay in play as digitalization evolves, but the time for transformation is now or executives will operate at sub-standard levels because of today's cost management lens coming short.

ACCOUNTING PILLARS

All companies face risk and uncertainty. Additionally, they all must decide on the information required to manage the enterprise. Three principal issues can be identified as the pillars of financial information that managers are given as aids to control activities and make decisions. First, as a business grows, the volume of production and activities tends to grow also. For just about any organization, the demand for products and services impacts costs and contributions to the bottom line. Accountants are adept in considering the relationships between profit, costs, and volume changes. They know how to assess costs that remain constant for extended periods of time and those that vary with production volume levels. Visualizing a business in terms of *scale* allows key decisions to be made, whether the firm is traditional in its operations or highly digitalized.

A second issue that enterprises face relates to the growth of their activities and the range of products that they offer. When increasing product and service range, the cost base of businesses grows, but not always in proportion to the increased units produced and delivered. In other words, an organization that diversifies its product range, will see increased resource utilization that is not a result of volume growth but instead that reflects changes in *scope*. So accounting tools have emerged to capture the scope effects of growth and ways of tracing cost increases to products, services, and activities that drive new costs. Again, digitalizing enterprises can benefit from the insights these tools can generate but some rethinking is necessary.

In Chapter 5, we'll look at a third pillar – that of learning curves for cost control. For now, we consider these two dimensions of accounting information and discuss the refocus required of the field to assist decision makers. Before we do that, though, we need to discuss a specific new form of risk, which finance leaders must acknowledge.

A RISK FROM WHICH THERE IS NO RETURN

For most people, risk assessment is a conditioned reflex in making decisions and taking action. Within organizations, the value of desired outcomes must be weighed against the costs of acting and the riskiness of outcomes. Less likely outcomes and unintended effects are evaluated, sometimes intuitively, though very often using complex mathematical and probabilistic estimates. All executives make decisions with a sense that the rewards should take account of the risks absorbed and they understand that a sure thing carries little risk and so, the payoffs can be anticipated to be smaller than those from a riskier proposition. What types of risks might an enterprise face? One is the *business risk* around the product, the technology, or the market. As such, there may be issues with the product if its quality, features, or delivery preferences do not meet expectations. There could be technological failings relating to development, provisioning, or servicing of the product.

At times, the customer segment being targeted will not be receptive to the product concept, or the market could shift too fast toward other solutions or just end up being too small in size. A company facing an unexpected increase in material or labor cost might have to make decisions based on market research and estimates of the costs of taking on the business risk. Technology decisions in particular are closely tied to business risk. Operating leverage affects a firm's business risk. For instance, if a company decides to invest in high-cost machinery, its fixed costs will rise. More fixed costs result in higher operating leverage, and thus, higher business risk. If the volume of sales declines after a company increases its operating leverage, the percentage of sales decline will be less than the percentage of profit decrease. This can thus be risky. But as might be expected, when sales are getting higher, the profit percentage growth is even higher. A second category of risk is *financial risk*. This is the risk that a company might not be able to meet its obligations and pay back its debts. The higher the level of debt taken by an enterprise, the higher the financial risk. So how the treasury function determines the funds requirements, and its sources will shape the level of financial risk of the firm.

These two types of risk permeate every business domain: markets, industries, and platforms, whether new and digitalizing or more traditional. But there exists a third type of risk affecting enterprises today. In fact, it is a form of risk that impacts business risk and financing risk as well. We'll call this *expertise risk*, which relates to not understanding changes that are influencing enterprises. Finance leaders are carriers of the greatest expertise risk facing enterprises. The inability to appreciate the pace and implications of digitalization and not delivering the right financial intelligence will either kill the enterprise or kill the accounting field itself!

Finance experts know that it is easier to execute in a market that already has existing acceptance of a product concept. Some firms, though, will mobilize an entirely new business model or develop a currently nonexistent one (the "dog" in Chapter 3). An attempt may be made for the product to have lock-in capability where there is resistance for customers to move away once they have understood and adopted the product's value after investing effort and time. If the concept enjoys network effects, the opportunity could lead to quick-paced business development and growth. Digital technologies, of course, evolve quickly and can fast become obsolete. Therefore, the loyalties of customers will alter just as rapidly as new disruptive technologies emerge.

What's more, in digital, most investment costs don't retain value after they've been incurred. Code can be expensive to create, and once developed, will hold minimal if any value at all. Unlike real assets such as buildings and land, digitalizing enterprises invest in costs that are of little use to others once incurred, and these costs tend to be high. Hardware costs themselves have to play catchup with technology advances. So fixed costs in digitalizing operations can be vast, and there is no comeback when things go wrong. They are *sunk*. Moreover, if products lack physical attributes, then production costs don't rise with sales volume growth, and pretty much all variable costs will be near-zero. Marginal costs tend to be low in digital and they tend to not increase with volume growth. Where service to users and customers are delivered by online agents such as robotic process automation (RPA) applications or AI machines, such costs, rather than being variable, will become fixed.

Thus, with digital, business risk may be extensive and operating leverage high. Financial risk may be mitigated if there is greater reliance on equity financing as a countermeasure. But expertise risk being high cannot be afforded. Not understanding business mechanics and the financial circuitry of digitalized operations can massively elevate expertise risk. Finance teams in this sense regulate expertise risk, and no business can come out alive by not managing high risk. Let's now turn to the pillars of financial information that managers are accustomed to.

VOLUME IS HALF THE STORY

A firm on a growth path will look to increasing the scale of its production. Much accounting expertise has had to do with how to forecast volume expansion; how to embed volume growth information into planning and budgets; working out ways of setting up purchasing and production functions so they can deal with volume changes; assessing what investments will meet demand growth in a cost- and capital-effective manner; and what is required financially to further expand markets. These are volume-focused accounting issues.

HOW BUSINESSES GENERATE PROFIT

A starting point to consider volume effects is, of course, to understand the mechanics of how a business generates profit. To assess profits, we need to be able to measure both our revenues and our costs. As we've noted, businesses may be traditional to the extent that the volume of business sales generates a closely tied level of costs because the products or services purchased by customers drive costs in an associated manner. Some digitalizing firms retain this characteristic. In other instances, a digital firm will have sources of revenues from customers, but its costs are incurred because of consumers whose needs must be serviced. Those needs may have little to do with the customers bringing in revenues. Naturally, by cost we mean a measure, in monetary terms, of what is given up by a business to acquire a product or a resource. These could be, for instance, utilities, packaging, delivery, and so on, which appear as expenses in the income statement. The accounting requirement is to represent such expenses matched up with sales revenues to work out the income for that period.

Firms tend also to have expenditures that help sustain the business. These types of costs remain unexpired and are classed as assets until they become expenses. They'll gradually lose value and future usefulness and become expensed. These relationships are useful to visualize in terms of the behavior of costs as operations take place. The expiration of some costs can be relatively variable, such as material expenses tied to production level, or electricity expenses to power a machine, or packaging expenses incurred as sales progress. Conversely, fixed costs remain constant in total terms. Clearly, not all costs vary in relation to volume of activity changes. Some alter with operational activities, and others remain constant. To keep things simple, accountants often assume no economies of scale effects in financial statements, but of course these can readily be incorporated – for instance, where the supply price of packaging material falls when a certain volume of purchases is achieved triggering a set discount. Accountants are adept at highlighting possible savings from bulk-buying. And they will also usually represent fixed and variable costs separately in statements so the decision maker can assess the impact of different costs on operations and decisions and also the trade-offs between variable and fixed costs.

In many instances, digital technologies lead to reductions in the use of labor input that directly varies with production. As firms invest in fixed costs, they often encounter lowered variable costs, which implies that different approaches can be deployed by a business in the production of goods and services and generating profits. Accounting reports, therefore, need to show how changing the mix of variable versus fixed costs has significance for strategic decisions about how much to invest in assets and of what types. For instance, many companies are implementing RPA systems where software tools act as virtual robots that automate certain transactional processes. RPAs can reduce direct labor cost inputs but being fixed costs in nature they will usually show up as overhead costs being incurred.

In making decisions and controlling operations, enterprises at some point are interested in knowing the revenues necessary to just match the total costs of carrying out operations. This, then, provides an indication of the total revenues or sales that are needed in order to attain the profit target desired. Naturally, where an enterprise runs at breakeven, it makes neither a profit nor a loss. Knowing the relationships between revenue, costs, and the capacity of the operations can prove highly useful. All we need to know are the estimated fixed costs for a future time period and the estimated variable costs over that same period. The accounting starting point is:

$$
\begin{aligned}
\text{Profit} &= \text{Sales} - \text{Costs} \\
&= \left(\text{Selling price per unit} \times \text{Quantity}\right) \\
&\quad - \left(\text{Variable costs} + \text{Fixed costs}\right)
\end{aligned}
$$

If Sales are equal in magnitude to Costs above, then the business is making no profit and the volume of activity is at *breakeven*. Naturally, the intent is to go beyond this point which implies that the *contribution* from operations (i.e., sales revenues less variable costs) goes further than just covering the fixed costs.

Digitalizing enterprises tend to have high fixed costs and, usually, this is countered by variable costs being lower. The changing cost mix evidenced by digitalizing firms implies that strategies unavailable to a company that produces using traditional means can be pursued because there are limits on how far variable costs can be lowered in such businesses. Digitalization implies cost structures that can be highly skewed toward fixed costs. Of note, however, is that the fixed costs are usually sunk in that they have already been incurred and can't be recovered. The variable costs, which become lower through digital, render increased contributions from each sale. This then leads to a need to decide what product prices to set and how to achieve market expansion. We can illustrate this as follows by comparing two digitalized enterprises operating in the high-tech sector.

MORE THAN JUST PROFIT

Suppose Super-Tech Company has developed a fiction-writing software called Super-Read. Super-Tech is about to begin marketing this new product. But, it has a competitor, Digi-Tech, which is also planning on launching its own software application called Digi-Story that can write fiction. Super-Tech sets the selling price for Super-Read at $80. It spends $2.8 million in development and online marketing costs in the first quarter. The software application also requires initial remote support, which costs $5 per unit. During the first quarter, Super-Tech sells 20,000 units of Super-Read. We can figure out Super-Tech's profit for the quarter:

$$\begin{aligned} \text{Profit} &= \text{Sales} - \text{Costs} \\ &= \left(\text{Selling price per unit} \times \text{Quantity}\right) \\ &\quad - \left(\text{Variable costs} + \text{Fixed costs}\right) \end{aligned}$$

so,

$$\begin{aligned} \text{Profit} &= \left(\$80 \times 20,000\right) - \left(\left(\$5 \times 20,000\right) + \$2,800,000\right) \\ &= -\$1,300,000 \end{aligned}$$

Super-Tech makes a loss of \$1.3 million in the first quarter.

Now, let's look at Digi-Tech's figures. It sells 25,000 units of its Digi-Story package during the same first quarter. Digi-Story is also priced at \$80. Digi-Tech's fixed costs for the quarter come to \$3.1 million, and its variable costs are \$4 per unit. So, for Digi-Tech, the profit level for the first quarter is:

$$\begin{aligned} \text{Profit} &= \left(\$80 \times 25,000\right) - \left(\left(\$4 \times 25,000\right) + \$3,100,000\right) \\ &= -\$1,200,000 \end{aligned}$$

Both Super-Tech and Digi-Tech incur losses during the first quarter of launch. During the next quarter, consumer interest in the product grows. Super-Tech achieves sales of 35,000 units of Super-Read. Digi-Tech, thanks to a successful digital marketing campaign, sells 240,000 units of Digi-Story. Both firms keep the price the same, at \$80, and they incur the same variable and fixed costs during the second quarter as they did in the first. For Super-Tech, then,

$$\begin{aligned} \text{Q2 profit} &= \left(\$80 \times 35,000\right) - \left(\left(\$5 \times 35,000\right) + \$2,800,000\right) \\ &= -\$175,000 \end{aligned}$$

The company still makes a loss, but a much smaller one than in the previous quarter.

In contrast, Digi-Tech's profit for the second quarter is:

$$\begin{aligned} \text{Q2 profit} &= \left(\$80 \times 240,000\right) - \left(\left(\$4 \times 240,000\right) + \$3,100,000\right) \\ &= \$15,140,000 \end{aligned}$$

The large volume of sales has produced a good profit level for Digi-Tech, and the company has a bigger share of the consumer market for the product. During the third quarter, customer sales rise very quickly for both firms. Super-Tech sells 300,000 units of Super-Read, and Digi-Tech sells 2,700,000 units of Digi-Story. The selling prices, variable costs, and fixed costs remain the same:

$$\text{Super-Tech's Q3 profit} = (\$80 \times 300,000)$$
$$- \big((\$5 \times 300,000) + \$2,800,000\big)$$
$$= \$19,700,000$$

and

$$\text{Digi-Tech's Q3 profit} = (\$80 \times 2,700,000)$$
$$- \big((\$4 \times 2,700,000) + \$3,100,000\big)$$
$$= \$201,100,000$$

By the third quarter then, Digi-Tech's profits are nine times those of Super-Tech. It is clear now that in the first year of operations, Digi-Tech's profits will be very high relative to Super-Tech's bottom line. Its market volume will grow, as will its market share. In the second quarter, Super-Tech did not get to break-even, while Digi-Tech had already gone on to achieve relatively high profits. It's true that very high fixed costs were incurred to start with, as the software product was being developed and refined, but sales helped cover these costs over time, and profits then rose extremely rapidly. The reason for the fast profit increase once past break-even point is that both firms had low variable costs and kept a fairly high selling price per unit. With a high contribution, once the fixed costs are covered, most of the revenues translate into cool profits. We started with:

$$\text{Profit} = \text{Sales} - \text{Costs}$$
$$= (\text{Selling price per unit} \times \text{Quantity})$$
$$- (\text{Variable costs} + \text{Fixed costs})$$

This translates into:

$$\text{Profit} = (\text{Contribution margin per unit} \times \text{Quantity}) - \text{Fixed costs}$$

where contribution margin per unit

$$= (\text{Selling price per unit} - \text{Variable cost per unit})$$

Now what if sales in the fourth quarter reach 600,000 units of Super-Read and 14 million of Digi-Story. Then the profits for the two companies are:

$$\text{Super-Tech's Q4 profit} = (\$75 \times 600,000) - \$2,800,000$$
$$= \$42,200,000$$

and

$$\text{Digi-Tech's Q4 profit} = (\$76 \times 14,000,000) - \$3,100,000$$
$$= \$1,060,900,000$$

$75 and $76 are the contribution margins for Super-Read and Digi-Story, respectively.

Super-Tech and Digi-Tech started out level but then Super-Tech lost volume sales and market presence. Digi-Tech could have advanced even faster in adjusting its pricing, just as could Super-Tech. When markets change fast and technologies advance rapidly, getting real-time information is important. Tech-based product markets can grow very quickly, so pursuing a strategy that is constantly being reviewed is vital. If Super-Tech does not quickly put in place some effective counter maneuvers during the first quarter, we've seen that it will be pushed out of the market by Digi-Tech. Digi-Story will try to *lock in* customers by enhancing the perception that the switching costs to a competitor product are high. Once in place, even if Super-Tech refines and develops Super-Read further such that it is a superior product to Digi-Story, Super-Tech probably won't be able to persuade customers to move over to Super-Read. They'll be locked into the Digi-Tech ecosystem. Few individuals who are used to Microsoft's OS have moved to Linux, which is open source and free. If Linux had been there first, things would look different today. Likewise, few would switch to an alternative keyboard layout like Dvorak that enable faster typing than the QWERTY setup because the latter has a deep lock on the market. In advanced digitalizing setting, fast decisions and action are crucial and, thus, accounting reporting that rapidly and effectively informs executive action must be in effect.

Pricing strategy is essential in thinking through market share growth. Both Super-Tech and Digi-Tech, could have reduced their selling price early to seek market share gain. Suppose Super-Tech and Digi-Tech both reduced their product prices. The contribution margin is $75 for Super-Read, and Digi-Tech's Digi-Story has a $76 contribution. Both offer huge room for price maneuvering which tends to be the case for digital products where very high contribution margins can exist – at least for a time. The two firms Super-Tech and Digi-Tech have high fixed costs, which will place intense pressure on reducing price in order to build market share rather than seeking to just break even as soon as possible. No incumbent firm can afford to let a competing product attain more market traction, as this becomes near impossible to reverse. The quick loss of market share to focus on rapidly rising profits is to be avoided.

If Super-Tech decides to drastically lower the price of Super-Read to $50 per unit, Digi-Tech can follow suit or perhaps price Digi-Story even lower at $35. Super-Tech might then match the price of Super-Read, or go lower still, to, say, $20. A price war would reflect both firms' intentions to sacrifice profits now so as to grow their market share. Conventionally, industrial firms would use full-cost calculations (i.e., the variable cost plus the fixed cost allocated per unit) and generally not go below this. Under some circumstances, there may be justification to go below the full cost. If the selling price is the same as the variable cost, then evidently break even cannot be achieved as no contributions go toward covering fixed costs. The losses for both firms would be the fixed costs incurred. With digital, low pricing, even below the variable cost can make sense to build the customer base. Some firms have been known to use negative pricing to build market presence faster than the competition.[5] After this, once a business is a market leader, it can normalize prices to deliver a profit.

Under digital, while traditional concepts of cost-volume-profit remain intact in terms of financial parameters, the implications for decision makers will alter because the coupling of management and finance has altered. Appropriate action in the face of the same financials in conventional industrial environments may not tally with what a digitalized enterprise might need to do. Therefore, financial information must be framed to enable effective decisions. The right accounting reporting is essential to benefit from technologies as they evolve, and this implies that accounting intelligence will need to be altered, too.

GROWTH THROUGH SCOPE

Enterprises over the past three decades have launched new products faster than ever. This has led product life cycles to become shorter and consumer tastes to also alter more rapidly. Much of this has been enabled by investments into flexible production systems, robotics, computer-integrated manufacturing, and reconfigurations of service environments. High hardware costs have resulted in huge investments, which in financial statements ultimately translate into overheads. While flexible organizational technologies have led to higher-volume production, their purpose has primarily been to increase the capacity for producing a larger range of products and services and to diversify product offerings. This has created difficulties for managers making product decisions where increased common costs and the sharing of resources by different products have to be properly allocated. Costing systems ill-equipped to provide information on how scope rather than volume drives costs have had to be rethought because technology ran ahead of accounting's ability to report effectively. Activity-based costing has been one response to dealing with this issue.

When accountants have overhead costs that need to be allocated to different products, they engage in *cost smoothing*! That is, they'll uniformly assign the costs of resources to products, services, and customers, even though individually these actually absorb resources in uneven ways. What then happens is that a product that requires a relatively high level of resources will be reported to have a low total cost of resource usage, and vice versa. A decision maker receiving a report showing a product's costs that are unknowingly *undercosted* and therefore supposedly profitable would likely place more resources toward selling that product. Naturally, if the product is in fact losing money unbeknownst to the executive, then this will result in revenues trailing the actual costs of the resources used in making that product.

For a product that is *overcosted*, the firm will be resistant to go below a certain selling price as this will result in perceived losses. The competition will offer a comparable product at lower prices that yield profits for them because they have a better understanding of the resource requirements for that product and are reporting this accurately. The firm will then back off from offering this product as it will appear to be loss making when in fact it brings in profits and will cut itself out of its market share, giving it away to the competition. In many cases, incorrect accounting information has led products to pull out of markets that are profitable because of poor financials, indicating that they're loss making. This has to do with broken costing systems rather than ineffective operations. In most instances, products actually cost less than what is reported in the accounts to management, and they could profitably be sold for less.

What actually happens when common costs are smoothed over many different products is that some products that do not tap into many resources end up subsidizing others that do. Usually, those produced in high volumes need less resources than low-volume, more-difficult-to-make products. Such product cost cross-subsidization is present when at least one mis-costed product causes the mis-costing of other products. An analogy would be when a diner is out with a group of three friends and eats and drinks much less than they do. That diner might get upset at having to pay for a bill that is averaged out across the four people! This is because the diner cross-subsidizes the others (and knows it). In enterprises, certain costs can be traced to products and services pretty directly, and the production volume correctly reflects the cost apportionment. But when common overhead costs get pooled and allocated in the same way, similarly to the diner, the product cost calculations have to be questioned if the products are very different in the resources they require. This is because it is the costs tied to product diversity and not volume that cause the cost increases in the first place. Volume of production is not a factor and does not cause the cost distortions. It is simply that different products draw on resources in differing ways so that some eat more resources and others less.

The way accountants have recently overcome many of the problems of costs allocations in diversified product environments is to refine costing systems by identifying individual activities such as designing products, setting up machines, operating production instruments, distributing products, and so on. *Activity-based costing* systems calculate the costs of individual activities and assign these on the basis of the activities undertaken to produce each product or service. The logic of activity-based costing systems is that more finely structured activity-cost pools with cost drivers lead to more accurate costing of activities. This recognizes that there is a cost hierarchy where a cost driver can be a unit of output such that volume of production reflects cost incurred. Or there may be many non–volume-related costs such as a group or batch that relates to a specific cost incursion for the whole batch. Recognizing these types of cost drivers affords activity-based costing much value in conventional business setups that require the costs of physical products and services to be accurately known (see Figure 4.1). Aside from batch-specific costs, there may also be product-sustaining costs, where resources sacrificed are due to activities undertaken to support individual products or services. Additionally there may even be facility-sustaining costs that require resources sacrificed on activities that cannot be traced to individual products or services but that support the organization and do not vary in any way with volume or scope of output.

One point to ponder is, how far should the penchant for cost allocation be retained in digitalized environments? Accounting professionals are well versed in cost allocation techniques. This expertise has served companies well when it was essential to allocate costs properly to internal activities and domains of production, so cost awareness and containment drives can be in effect in enterprises. But this is inappropriate where business viability and growth have to be prioritized through digital means. In such contexts, we cannot

Figure 4.1 When ABC is useful.

promote cost allocation mechanisms just to provide comfort that technical accounting exigencies have been met. If cost determinations are premised on past financial plumbing structures, then these will act as barriers to a responsive digital future. The finance function has to hold back on mandating cost calculation symmetries that resonate with good conventional accounting wisdom but which jettison organizational adeptness and growth in digital. Of essence are intelligent digitalization outcomes that propel the business model rather than cost calculation protocols that are there to satisfy the traditional accounting mind-set.

If it is established that some level of accuracy is desirable in working out product costs, then the question might be asked as to whether activity-based costing, which has been successful in tallying costing systems accuracy with innovative technologies that permit greater product diversity, can be useful in digitalizing enterprises. What needs to be asked is: Are there non-volume costs that rise with product diversity? If so, then activity-based costing approaches can be useful. If digital technologies such as IoT, blockchain, AI, cloud accounting, and others are used within manufacturing, retail, financial, hospitality, and service settings, which are transitioning in the way they carry out their operations, then activity-based costing will aid in identifying cost source points and in determining the costs of products, services, and processes with greater accuracy. This is because competitive markets demand product diversity and fast evolution, and these costs can be differentiated into volume-based and non–volume-driven costs, which will prove useful in decisions (see Figure 4.2).

Many business environments will be undergoing digital transformations in the short term, such that operations are automated but the products and services are physical. In such instances, activity-based

Figure 4.2   ABC is less useful in digital.

costing's potential for effectively accounting for products and services in terms of their costs of production will be reduced. This arises because automated processes and digitalized activities including robotized decision-making must be left in cost pools that should not enter costing calculations. They simply cannot be tied to specific cost-driving activities other than arbitrarily so. Overuse of any costing system where costs are difficult to assign rationally will lead to incorrect decisions if reliance is placed on costings in making decisions. In the case of digitalized operations producing digital products, costs do not generally increase with non–volume-driven factors. Scale effects, in other words, will likely not feature to a great extent in driving costs, and so activity-based costing applied to products and services will fail to provide insightful information. If, for instance, coding enables service or product diversification, then these are likely fixed costs incurred on an ongoing basis to refine and alter production continuously. Seeking to capture and allocate these costs to individual products and services may make little sense, as coding may be enabling the delivery of more diverse products but coding activity does not directly drive costs. Cost accuracy is likely to be less relevant than information gained from the market, leading to product refinements. Such refinements will take place rapidly, and concomitant decisions will be taken that would only be hampered if arbitrary cost allocations were part of managerial reports. The business model premised on the delivery of digital products will determine what accounting information is relevant, but it is unlikely that product diversity would cause cost increases if many of the activities are powered by truly fixed costs that do not tie into scale or scope effects.

It is important to note that activity-based costing is not solely about attempting to gain costing accuracy. The information may be used to identify and track non–value-added activities that an enterprise might be seeking to eliminate over time. It may also be highly useful as part of performance management systems where cost-driver metrics are tracked and evaluated at a business unit or managerial level. Broadly speaking, as an enterprise shifts from having physical products, physical processes, and physical agents toward digital products, digital processes, and digital agents, the value of costing techniques such as activity-based costing that focus on capturing scope effects becomes less significant (see Figure 4.3).

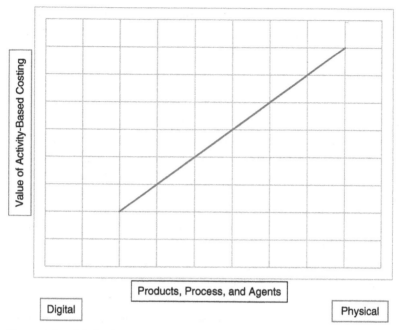

Figure 4.3 Digitalization and the value of activity-based costing.

We've seen that volume and scope changes impact cost calculations. Much of this has usefully been acknowledged by accountants who've developed techniques to deal with business environments that became more complex. Accounting professionals are today well versed in cost allocation techniques. This expertise has served companies well when it was essential to allocate costs properly to internal activities and elements of production for certain decisions. But where business viability and growth have to be prioritized through digital means, this can go too far. In such contexts, we cannot privilege cost allocation methodologies over digital evolution just to provide comfort that technical accounting exigencies have been afforded. If cost determinations are premised on past financial plumbing precepts, then these will act as barriers to enterprise growth. The finance function has to hold back on mandating cost calculation symmetries that resonate with good conventional accounting wisdom but that jettison organizational adeptness and agility. Of primary essence should be intelligent digital outcomes that advance the business model, rather than cost calculation protocols that are there to reassure the technical accounting mind-set. We consider in Chapter 5 how experience shapes costs and, more importantly, how learning from data supercharges digitalizing organizations.

NOTES

1. IHS Markit. 2020. BP CEO Bernard Looney on creating a "lighter, more agile, more focused" organization; energy transition and net zero carbon emissions by 2050; operating in today's oil market and why shale is really a "tech business." Press release. http://news.ihsmarkit.com/prviewer/release_only/ slug/bizwire-2020-6-11-bp-ceo-bernard-looney-on-creating-a-lighter-more-agile-more-focused-organization-energy-transition-and-net-zero-carbon-emissions-by-2050-operating-in-todays-oil-market-and-why-shale-is-really-a-tech-business

2. Amadeo, K. 2020. Oil price history – Highs and lows since 1970: What makes oil prices so volatile. *The Balance* (April 22). https://www.the balance.com/oil-price-history-3306200

3. Gordon, P. 2020. Norwegian oil and gas giant Equinor appoints Anders Opedal as new CEO. *Smart Energy International* (August 11). https://www .smart-energy.com/industry-sectors/business/norwegian-oil-and-gas-giant-equinor-appoints-anders-opedal-as-new-ceo/

4. Digitalization helps oil producers wring out profits, even in hard times. 2020. *Bloomberg NEF* (March 25). https://about.bnef.com/blog/ digitalization-helps-oil-producers-wring-out-profits-even-in-hard-times/

5. Bhimani, A. 2017. *Financial Management for Technology Start-Ups: A Handbook for Growth*. Kogan Page.

CHAPTER **5**

Learning Is Everything

When the rate of change outside is more than what is inside, be sure that the end is near.
                                   —Azim Premji, chairman, Wipro Limited

In 1922, T. P. Wright, who later co-founded the Curtiss-Wright Corporation, became interested in the cost of making airplanes.[1] He pondered how it might be possible to satisfy an order by the Bureau of Air Commerce for 10,000 two-seater airplanes at $700 each, given that the production costs per unit were much higher than this. He reported in the *Journal of the Aeronautical Sciences* that aircraft manufacturers could observe employee hours required to assemble planes going down as the number of planes produced increased. Wright observed that learning took place in a manner that was not random and that one could in fact work out quite accurately how much labor time would be required to build planes at different points in time depending on the number of planes already built. Thus, it would be a mere calculation to find out the profitability of selling this many planes, knowing that at the outset the selling price was below cost but profits would quickly ensue. During the World War II years, government contractors regularly applied Wright's idea that experience in production can be used to obtain estimates of the timing and costing for vehicles, planes, and ship construction at different volumes of overall production.

Accountants are fully aware that organizations develop knowledge about practices that continuously improve as production takes place, which then has cost impacts that follow specific patterns. This is because with practice comes the realization that things can be done better and more efficiently. So with volume of activity, cost reductions can arise not just from classical scale economies but also from *learning* how to do more with less and doing it better. A firm that is aware of the value of prior experience can develop an edge in its pricing, investment, marketing, and diversification decisions. Harnessing learning effects can prove remarkably important in digital business contexts. We focus on learning what learning does in digital here.

LEARN FAST: CUT COSTS FASTER

It is well known that repeating a task can lead to a better output if one refines how the task is carried out over time. We've known, in fact, that costs come down in a precise mathematical fashion as repetitive tasks are performed because of increases in efficiency. Continuously producing a particular product yields insights on how to reduce the material being used or scrapped, how to carry out operational activities more efficiently, how to restructure processes so less labor is required for a given level of output, and so on. In other words, cost reductions are closely associated with the knowledge gained from action. Most industries today have executives thinking about product pricing where an expectation exists that experience with production can lead to lower costs. Accountants took time to warm up to reporting on learning curve effects in analyses prepared for decision makers. But now they regularly apply this understanding to costing calculations to provide executives information about cost behavior changes that accrue as a result of the organizational knowledge base growing. We want to look at mathematically what makes learning so powerful when enterprises go digital.

Technically, we can think of the learning curve as follows: Suppose a unit within a business that designs websites has an 80% learning curve as experience accrues in constructing sites of a specific design type and specifications. We might start by saying that the website product initially needs 1,000 hours for the first one, but then the second website with a similar construct and structure requires less time and the overall cumulative average time is 800 hours. In other words we have an 80% learning rate from the initial 1,000 hours, so 1,000 hours was spent on the first website plus only 600 hours for the second website, resulting in a total of 1,600 hours divided by two websites giving the 800 hour average. Learning at the same rate will, following the fourth website, bring the cumulative average time to 640 hours (that is, 80% of 800 hours). And then after the eighth website, the cumulative average will go down to 512 hours (that is, 80% of 640 hours). So we can see that the total time to finish off eight websites will be 4,096 hours (that is, eight websites multiplied by the average time of 512 hours). We could generically apply the following formula:

$$T_n = T_1 n^b$$

where,

n = the unit number (1 for the first unit of the product, 2 for the second unit, etc.)

T_1 = the amount of time to produce the first unit of the product

T_n = the amount of time to produce unit n

b = the learning curve index (log learning curve percentage $p \div \log 2$)

l = the learning percentage

So b for an $l = 80\%$ curve would be log $0.8 \div \log 2 = -0.322$.

What we see here is that to complete a website, the learning as websites are constructed entails a reduction of 20% every time volume of production doubles. This is our 80% learning curve, of course. So learning curves reveal that the cumulative average time per unit declines by a constant percentage each time the cumulative quantity of units produced doubles. In our example, we know that when the quantity of websites designed is doubled from X to $2X$, the cumulative average time per unit for the $2X$ units is 80% of the cumulative average time per unit for the X units. In other words, average time per unit has dropped by 20%. We can also think of learning whereby the incremental unit time (how long is needed to produce the last unit) declines by a constant percentage each time the cumulative

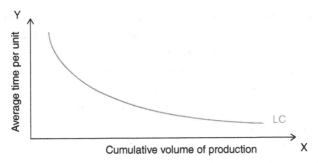

Figure 5.1 The learning curve – time to produce vs. cumulative production.

quantity of units produced doubles. The 80%, in other words, implies that when the quantity of units produced doubles from X to $2X$, the time required to produce the last unit at the $2X$ production level is considerably lower than the time needed to produce the last unit at the X production level. Graphically, Figure 5.1 reveals the effect of a learning curve where average production time per unit decreases as the total accumulated production rises.

Conventionally, the learning curve effect has been useful in estimating costs at any volume production point, and helps establish the selling price as explained by Mr Wright. We might have a company that sets a very low selling price on its product to drive high demand. As the company's production increases to meet the growing demand for its product, the costs per unit decline. The enterprise rides the product down the learning curve while generating a higher market share. Although it earns little or no profit on its first unit sold, it will eventually generate greater profit per unit as its output increases. This explains the many claims of predatory pricing by domestic companies pointing to foreign firms selling products in markets at below cost using subsidies that fall foul of trade regulations. This is done by these firms in the knowledge that the volume of sales ultimately will lead to profitability on units sold past a point without the need for further subsidies that benefits both producers and consumers (and the foreign competitor).

INTELLIGENT LEARNING

Because the combination of AI learning dynamics and finance is so crucial to succeeding in digitalizing environments, it is worthwhile for finance leaders to spend time considering the mechanics of learning curve effects and recognizing that learning curves are nonlinear. A learning curve can display how resource consumption can decline or for instance, how price changes adjust in reaction to consumer trends as agents learn and become better at fine-tuning prices. In physical operational environments, managers learn how to improve the scheduling of work shifts and plant operators learn how to best operate the facility, and so on. The learning curve notion can be extended to include other activities in the value chain, including marketing, distribution, customer service, and supply chain flows. In many instances, unit costs decrease as productivity increases. These relationships are nonlinear.

What is clear is that thinking individuals learn when they repeat tasks. They need less time to produce as they become more adept and familiar with what is required. This applies also to the material wasted, which then goes down as more production experience is gained. What happens in learning curve contexts is that the cumulative average time per unit is reduced by a defined level as the cumulative output doubles. But the effect of the learning rate in relation to time taken loses impact as production increases. It will likely ultimately become negligible. In Figure 5.1, it is evident that Mr. Wright's learning effect is very high at the outset but the line becomes horizontal after a while.

Now if we fast-forward to the present, repetitive tasks can be automated, especially in relation to accounting. Robotic process automation (RPA) systems can ground procedures and activities that need to be carried out repetitively with much efficiency. The algorithms can be altered as evidence arises on the effects of RPA, such that activities become more fine-tuned in meeting output needs. Where we use AI, the learning occurs as data is analyzed and operations take place. The machine learns with more data points and actions. This learning can occur with the same volume effects as with Mr. Wright's airplane analogy; however, the learning is embedded in the algorithms. Consequently, volume of activity feeds output relevance. This is virtuous learning. If AI agents respond to changing markets and volume distribution in the marketplace through repricing, then learning can take place in relation to the pricing alterations. More refined pricing vis-a-vis volume and other factors implies great value creation possibilities for customers and this will drive sales and profit. With AI and machine learning, the effectiveness of machine-based output improves. The endgame is to learn faster than the competition using both sales and costs, which, as explained in Chapter 4, may relate to different stakeholders – customers as well as clients.

AI can tap into learning effects to create fast-paced growth. The faster enterprises can learn from data about machine actions and continuously assess the consequences of further actions in a loop, the sooner they can home in on appropriate ways of managing costs, setting prices, and undertaking marketing action. The effects become circuitous as the volume of activities undertaken triggers more data from which learning emanates leading to more volume growth. A positive virtual cycle of action, data, and learning producing more action is enabled by AI technologies (see Figure 5.2). Mr. Wright's learning calculus places this cycle on steroids. Data in digitalized operations contexts do not take long to double in cumulative terms relative to the physical production of goods. Competitors with less data and activity sets will trail. They'll be less adept because they'll be slower to learn, which will make them even less adept by reducing the data they can access. This, in turn, will slow their learning capacity.

In digital, the learning effects snowball very rapidly. This makes large and smart market players more adaptive. Darwin's adage that those who survive are the ones who most accurately perceive their

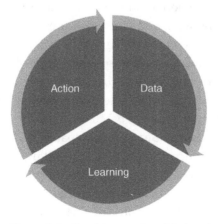

Figure 5.2 The virtuous action-data-learning cycle.

environment and successfully adapt to it holds true. More important, if finance leaders are unable to grasp the relevance of information reflective of the new learning curve workings where AI systems operate, then enterprises with real potential to thrive will lose out to competitors who who adapt faster.

PUSH THE PEDAL

Across enterprises, we have seen that digital technologies are influencing management practices and decisions. Evidence from global surveys suggests that the most tangible benefits from AI implementations include improved operational efficiency and cost savings, enhanced management decision-making, and better customer experience.[2] Increased revenue, faster time to market, and more effective risk management also result from AI investments. But the benefits of digital are to be reaped by those who understand that digitalization requires a mind-set change in relation to financial management practices and processes. For this reason, this book has argued for the need to assess and learn how to extract what can benefit a digitalizing organization from our existing financial management toolbox and rethink what tools need changing. Importantly, there is a need to be careful not to discard practices wholesale where what is needed is simply fine-tuning.

All the evidence we have indicates that going digital offers potential of a magnitude unseen in the history of business. This makes digital transformation a boon for any corporate leader. But the financial circuitry of highly digitalized enterprises can also be their bane. Not seeing the financial control pedals that must be pushed will kill many industry incumbents. Enterprises that adopted activity-based costing decades ago to capture the scope effects associated with the then new technologies were better able to survive and thrive in competitive markets. Without activity-based costing, these firms could not make effective decisions. Similarly, companies today that understand the accounting underpinnings of digital will use this knowledge to get to very high profits through sounder and more adept moves and deliver value to customers that exceeds what other market players will achieve. But the reasons for these payoffs are quite different to those from the activity-based costing context. It is not to do with greater accuracy of costing which leads to better production, marketing, pricing, and other decisions. Accuracy is not of the essence, the cost structure is for one, more relevant to appreciate in digital. Adding a customer in digital enterprises adds minimal variable costs if any at all, relative to having interactions between the customer and a human agent. This makes the scalability potential very large with digital. Indeed, variable costs tend to decrease extensively as repetitive tasks get automated and AI-powered operating mechanisms take over or replace managerial functions concerned with designing, tracking, supervision, and so on with less human error. Add to this that faster decisions get taken with greater effectiveness due to learning effects. Selling prices could be sustained in growth markets when competitors are few and the product concept takes hold. Under such circumstances, the low variable costs will magnify contribution margins. Knowledge as to accurate variable or other costs will not drive better decisions. What *will* is that AI agents can process market data and muster growth through tactical marketing and pricing ploys, in part because of the nature of variable costs rather than extreme cost accuracy.

Of importance is that the fundamental strategy of the business model must be part of the equation for any enterprise making decisions in such a situation. Rather than seize high yield right away, the big contributions that could be had should perhaps instead drive executives to enjoy the flexibility they have at hand to reduce prices and detract competitors in order to achieve a larger market presence ultimately. The attendant data from such a maneuver will drive more such moves from more data in continuous time. The strategic insight to make decisions like these cannot be entirely left to algorithms. It is the finance team's job to apprise decision makers of the possibilities and to do so in real time.

Aside from the particularity of variable cost characteristics, fixed costs can be very high in digital but are not recoupable for the most part. The presence of large sunk costs due to technology investments that are worthless outside the context of the company will engender a managerial sentiment that if things go wrong, assets cannot be sold. The path to profitability that decision makers see when variable costs stay constant and very low combined with fixed costs that are sunk and very high, is very possibly to pursue market growth with greater fervor. This means pursuing long-run high profitability, possibly at the cost of short-term losses for the enterprise. Conventionally, few firms would chase growth in the absence of profits over any time frame. It is the specific low variable costs/high fixed costs structure of digital enterprises that inherently drives many toward putting growth before profit. Such strategic choices cannot be left to machines but also could not have been available for human decision makers to ponder without machines!

To add to this, in situations where network effects can be leveraged, the intent should be to reach a threshold user volume at which point accelerated market growth is mobilized and fast-rising demand for the product offering is triggered. This is important in markets where room only exists for a few large players. In certain very narrow market segments, some firms will operate where there's either a lot of slack or unused capacity that can be put to use if the right technical infrastructure is in place. Then, a product innovation (like Uber or Airbnb) can grow, making the traditional players (taxis and hotels) less attractive, and the most adept firms will exclude others to take the lion's share of the business. There won't be much more room than for a few players, as much of the gains that old-industry incumbents used to access get redistributed to customers and a slice of the pie goes to the innovating firms. Where prices paid by consumers goes down, the market attracts a higher band of consumers and expands. And as more consumers get attracted to the product, much of that economic value created ends up going to the digitalized innovator. For these reasons, highly digitalized firms will seek to initially sacrifice profit pursuits to prioritize market share growth. They'll introduce innovative product features and try to disrupt through branding initiatives and garden fencing customers, and so on as much as possible. Digitalization enables paths to growth, but the right information is required for strategic moves to be made. For some products, it is the case that the last firms standing will make most of the money because "winner takes all" is potentialized by the cost structure of digitally transformed firms, as noted earlier. Those that know how to grow will grow fastest, to the exclusion of others. Such knowledge rests on financial information that captures the wider implications of the new technologies for effectively driving the enterprise. Ultimately, the new technology is about enabling better strategizing, and possibly monopolizing market segments. This is being achieved with greater knowledge from different data sources, enhanced insights from networked systems, and a better understanding of the financial circuitry underpinning the business, rather than cost accuracy and the pursuit of competencies drawn from analog-age organizational thinking.

NOTES

1. Wright, T. P. 1936. Factors affecting the cost of airplanes. *Journal of the Aeronautical Sciences* 3. http://www.uvm.edu/pdodds/research/papers/others/1936/wright1936a.pdf
2. Schmelzer, R. 2020. AI adoption survey shows surprising results. *Forbes* (January 23). https://www.forbes.com/sites/cognitiveworld/2020/01/23/ai-adoption-survey-shows-surprising-results/#f97d04b55e93

CHAPTER **6**

Performance
Changes

With the mass adoption of new technologies and disruptive work models, relying on now obsolete concepts of leadership is no longer effective for the management of people.[1]

—Yogesh Sirohi, CFO, PwC India

Development Bank of Singapore (DBS) is the largest bank in Singapore and Southeast Asia. Over 10 years ago, it had mediocre credit card application structures, its relationships managers had a high level of turnover, its branches and ATMs suffered long lines, and its customer satisfaction scores trailed behind those of its competitors. The bank's CEO and chief data officer began a strategy to make DBS "digital to the core."[2] For that to happen, a culture change was required that would bolster the digital innovation trajectory. Performance management had to tie into the problems the bank was experiencing. The bank set targets through the use of technology, and process changes achieving results far exceeding what it anticipated including a 25-fold higher reduction in customer wait hours. DBS has since developed its own mobile payment solution for customers; uses big data analyses in tracking potential trade fraud and in working capital management; deploys blockchains in letters of credit exchanges; and is evolving its AI systems to keep the bank ahead of changing market conditions, technical innovations, and the resultant emerging needs of its customers. The group head of Global Transaction Services at DBS, John Laurens,[3] sees this process as being about "transforming the way industries work by providing greater transparency, security and speed to build trade ecosystems."

In the era of digitalization, we have made a case for being agile, innovative, breaking from the past, reloading, building tomorrow, creating 2.0, while we think about 3.0, and so on. Yet, human nature is such that we like to compare before acting. We determine where we want to be in relation to where we've come from and we assess where we should be going by taking account of information on hand. Moreover, we want to compare where we got to relative to where we thought we might be. In financial terms, where we go has tended to be dictated by where we've been historically and where others are now. Much of the time, we work out variances between plans and actual outcomes. Organizational performance evaluation almost invariably engages comparisons with projections that capture results and growth over time. All investors, managers, and employees see positive performance in terms of progress over time and meeting or exceeding targets. Financial statements speak to results and comparisons over time periods that allow performance to be tracked. Planning implicitly involves setting expectations *ex-ante* so we can gauge whether *ex-post* performance matches/exceeds those expectations. The focus tends to be always on results achieved as time passes. This is in need of revision – performance management cannot follow just this perspective in the era of digitalization.

Much of digital is about altering what exists today to take advantage of possibilities that were not there or could not be seen yesterday. The priority has become to better understand how the state of play can be more comprehensively analyzed and acted on to produce a different future. Financial growth underlies measurements relative to the past, while digital evolution has to gauge something much bigger. That something has to be made visible from information analyses so that we get insights on how to achieve novel outcomes. Effective decisions in digitalized contexts rely on assessments of multiple sources of information not all of which reflect where we've been since we need to go where we've not been before! Certainly, good financial performance remains a goal to be pursued and expectations still need to be set to grow larger returns. The two are not contradictory. They're just different facets that need to be understood to move ahead. Relationships between the past, present, and future have to be analyzed to bring home outcomes valued by investors, workers, customers, and a myriad of other stakeholders. The lens that can help finance teams needs to be refocused but not jettisoned.

Conventionally, enterprise executives have been charged with managerial issues such as maximizing ROI, ensuring cost containment, enhancing quality of service and products, increasing customer satisfaction, growing market share, being avant-garde and innovative, positively engaging the workforce, demonstrating care for the environment, and upholding corporate responsibilities, as well as adhering to regulations and corporate governance parameters and vying for corporate leadership across a multitude of planes. Does any of this need to change in the new digital economy we have entered? No – absolutely not. But how we achieve all this and develop further aims has to alter. We don't want to throw out the finance baby with dated bathwater, as much corporate wisdom is mounted on sound structures that have to be retained. Rethinking and altering finance expertise requires understanding of the digital world we have entered rather than total amputation and dismemberment. What is surfacing from digitalized enterprises is that how we assess performance and reward it when warranted is changing. We discuss performance management issues here. We'll see that performance assessment systems will need to encompass learning, developing, and fostering essential capabilities and skills, and engaging in cultural change.

NEW TARGETS FOR PERFORMANCE MANAGEMENT

Some enterprises have started to replace current performance evaluation systems that rest on financial and accounting metrics because they view these as no longer being applicable in situations where workers need to aim for creative actions, learn new things, and create novel solutions. The shift is one that moves away from periodic appraisals using standard metrics toward informal feedback and evaluations of performance. But the evidence from many digitalizing enterprises points to some formal performance appraisal mechanisms remaining key in promoting individual innovation and creativity in workplaces.[4] The answer is to assess how far financial metrics relating to enterprise-wide performance continue to perform as evaluation mechanisms. As digitalizing enterprises experiment with different approaches to performance assessment, some broad macro-factors must be considered. These relate to shifts in the nature of work contracts toward contingent workers, the global talent shortage, lessons learned from the COVID-19 pandemic, alterations in global supply chain logistics, capacity and reliance, and the changing nature of work itself aside from technological advances.

WHOSE PERFORMANCE, ANYWAY?

The constitution of the workforce is changing in enterprises. Many are millennials and many more are Generation Z individuals. Millennial workers like to see the existence of development opportunities and seek work experiences that give meaning. They prefer environments that are congenial. The upcoming Generation Z has different expectations from work life and the organizations they work in. We have noted that Gen Zers have a tendency to be always connected. They prioritize the self in relation to testing things, are open to altering their perspectives and experimenting. They analyze much more information than preceding generations. But they do so differently because technology has placed a vast level of information before them aside from having shaped their habits. They are also more analytical and subscribe to the idea of balanced pragmatism in their assessments of information. They process different information types of varying provenance which arrive at different times and speed. As information enables them to better define their identity, it also lets them feel in control. They are self-learners who especially shape their knowledge base from online channels and sources.

Gen Zers have vast amounts of information at their disposal, and they are more pragmatic and analytical about their decisions than members of previous generations were. Moreover, they show a preference for experiences more than for ownership and tend toward business models that give them access to a range of experiences as workers. Rather than viewing consumption in terms of products, they regard them more as services that engender more connections. To feel engaged and integrated and part of the community, Gen Zers value connections that intensify information exchanges. These characteristics imply a need for performance management systems that emphasize different elements, depending on the composition of the workforce. Performance management systems can never stand still!

OPERATIONS GET CLOSER TO STRATEGY

Many performance appraisal systems are based on outcomes achieved relative to predetermined targets. And there is evidence that where these are used, they can be effective in promoting innovation. This aligns with what we know about having clear and measurable outcomes that identify the results to be pursued by employees. Clarity as to how outcomes are assessed and monitored encourages people to move toward achieving those outcomes because there is commitment reflective of what the enterprise signals as being important in a transparent and understandable manner. Accounting measures of performance attainment tend to highlight the objectives aimed for and the calculations that will be tied to depicting the results achieved, and this remains fully the case in motivating individuals in digitalizing enterprises. So it is to be anticipated that performance appraisal systems will be regarded as fair if they are results focused and comprehensible. But when performance is closely linked to payoffs for employees, there can also be a tendency to encourage targeting quantifiable short-term achievements that gives credence to the achievement of small adjustments and increments that echo past ways of working. How do we then get individuals to act so as to bring about innovations with high impact in the short and longer term, rather than just encourage small incremental successes that conventional performance management systems tend to emphasize? We will see here that part of the solution lies in rethinking activities to be pursued without necessarily referring to what is strategic and what is operational. This is a mind-set change on a grand scale requiring an easily overlooked but crucial alteration in how we visualize and assess digital enterprise setups.

If finance teams deploy conventional financial monitors of performance while more closely integrating short term moves and longer-term strategic intent, it would be erroneous to do what industrial age enterprises have done when the level of uncertainty in the environment rises. That is, to increase metrics and indicators of desirable performance as organizational uncertainty grows more complex in order to retain control. Such an approach can instigate large-scale errors for digitalizing organizations because it discourages actions and adjustments on the fly by those best able to gauge their appropriateness. Muting uncertainty through financial and managerial controls is not the answer in digital, because it is in the capture and analysis of ongoing changes that forward paths get created. In practice, what is preferable is to let employees develop the competences they need and let them put these skills into effect in pursuing innovation and creativity. Hanging onto conventional controls and indicators that provide adequate oversight as greater autonomy of action is accorded is fine. But in digital enterprises, individuals should not be chided for deviating from predetermined goals established by others, where setting self-targets can better lead to real growth.

Industrial Age control beliefs hold that the standard setter should not be the worker who is to be incentivized to achieve those standards. This has changed in digital. Individuals should in many cases, be setters of their own task-specific standards. Moreover, this should be so very often as action is engaged in. They should be judged on achieving parameters they have established themselves, which meet the wider, more generic and overarching financial and accounting targets the enterprise is moving toward. In this way, innovation and creativity of action that are highly prized in digitalized companies are encouraged and intelligently pursued at the individual level precisely because conventional norms of what is to be expected are adhered to only in broader terms and specific actions are pursued by those best placed to achieve them. The principal task for the finance function is now to have a proper understanding of the mind-set of workers that makes digital operations successful while also maintaining financial accountability.

INCENTIVIZING DIGITALIZATION

Evidence from enterprises is surfacing that performance evaluation mechanisms that stress the development of new competencies that individuals themselves develop as they perform their activities enhances their innovative and creative capacities – qualities that digitalizing organizations value. Altering the assessment of individuals goes beyond performance evaluation systems catching up with new technological realities. It has been reported that ". . . performance appraisal that boosts employees' innovation at work may . . . further foster digitalization."[5] In other words, enterprises that align their performance evaluation controls to their digitalization drive enhance their digital progress!

In our example of the Development Bank of Singapore, key to the organizational, technological, and cultural changes to deal with the problems faced by the bank, was to change the way performance was managed. There had to be a frame of understanding that took account of the problems the bank was experiencing, such as the low level of customer satisfaction. The customer-wait time had to be reduced, which determined targets to be set that took account of the digital technologies in use. But there was also reliance on an altering culture of involvement in evaluating performance. It is this that would allow much higher achievements to materialize than initially thought. The CEO and CDO looked at the competition in wider terms as not only coming from existing banks but also fintech startups and other providers of bank-like services and products. They also decided to reengineer DBS based on how companies like Facebook, Alibaba, Netflix, and Amazon regarded their internal systems. The key to the transition was to take account of the workforce characteristics, the bank's internal culture, the digital technologies in use, and the wider competition from within the industry and further afield.

The bank applied a conventional comparative perspective in assessing its performance using numbers to signal what it wanted to achieve and then measuring its activities vis-a-vis those goals. On the face of it, this was no different from what traditional performance evaluation systems undertake to do. The defining factor, however, is that the enterprise had to reinvent itself in relation to the technology available and couple this to a companywide culture change coming into effect. Just like Jeff Bezos, who famously desires an empty seat at meetings to represent the perspective of the customer, DBS had to internalize and envision the customer journey in order to remove all elements of friction across every decision relating to process changes giving the customer a pivotal role. It is well known that digital customers of financial institutions enable higher income generation relative to traditional customers because technological capacity, once established can service large-scale customer requirements at lower incremental costs. DBS paid heed to this. Within a few years, the results of the changes put into effect led DBS to become a banking leader in the digital age. The bank altered what needed to be done by continuously redefining internal processes and targets but maintaining its eye on financial growth and return performance parameters. Its operational indicators kept a focus on calculative metrics such as how quickly customers would migrate to digital banking services, how much time they waited, what resources they required that impacted the financials, and so on.

Important to understanding the success of DBS is that the bank has had access to a highly educated and skilled workforce. To counter gaps in employees' digital adeptness or fill a need to enhance certain skills, the bank established an online learning platform with courses that would help individuals develop specific digital banking skills. This included various categories such as journey thinking, digital communications, business models, as well as risk assessment, agility, and controls. An expectation existed amongst bank employees that their initiative will be rewarded not just financially but also in terms of being able to maximize the autonomy that digital technologies can afford in situations where an individual can put into action decisions they are given the autonomy to take and that reflect the information they can access in real time.

DBS used a balanced scorecard to track its progress across various dimensions with digital transformation being the most salient element. In fact, DBS tied 20% of the bank's performance to digitalization effects using precise metrics. So, for instance, DBS would monitor the proportion of customers who were acquired digitally and it would for every product or service establish targets for customer shifts toward electronic channels. A link was partly made to individuals' remuneration packages. But DBS decided that it would retain its annual appraisal process with KPIs that are identified for individuals to try and meet and once these targets are established great autonomy is provided without superior intervention and often in the absence of closely associated financial incentives. The bank made efforts to create a digitalization enhancing culture organizationally but it went further. It created co-creative hubs whereby customers are themselves made to be digitally more adept. Customer care representatives would work with customers to resolve issues they faced, and the help required by customers as they matured digitally was monitored. Dashboards captured digital data of interactions between customer care representatives and the customers they assisted. Over time, customers called the bank to resolve issues that online tools could not deal with, and this led to digitalization improvements in the bank's services, which kept it ahead of the competition. Such drives led DBS to become Global Finance's Best Bank in the World within a decade. And all this happened before DBS's push to deploy machine learning and advanced analytics tools to increase optimized customer interactions.

DATA'S CONSEQUENCES

There are instances of organizations that will use AI management systems invasively and instrumentally because of the potential they offer for tracking workers. For instance, some companies collate data on tasks performed by workers based on their browsing history, emails, chats, and periodic screenshots of workers' monitor displays.[6] The sentiments expressed in communications are also tracked with natural language processing tools. The data is then aggregated by a machine learning agent, which identifies anomalous behaviors, following which nudging or warning messages may be sent to the workers who do not follow norms. The monitoring approach aided by software-driven ranking and assessment may also be linked to remuneration, promotion potential, or disciplinary action.

At times, digital technologies have been used to shape the behaviors of workers. Some companies use systems to monitor workers in ways they are not aware of, or which they would not ordinarily have opted for. It is not difficult to deploy machine learning tools to work out behavioral patterns both within and after work hours. Such information can then enable actions to alter worker behavior or increase productivity or exploit profit enhancement moves. The impact may be adverse and can lead to other unintended costs for companies. When a business has much data at its disposal, it may engage in exploring avenues to enhance profit making in ways not known or favored by workers. Uber, for instance, investigated the behavior of its drivers to see if their actions could be modified using data analytics. It is in Uber's favor to have many available cars on the road even when demand is low and drivers will take home less earnings. Drivers have a tendency to set themselves specific income targets, at which point they stop working. Looking at the data sources at its disposal, Uber worked out that drivers will relinquish earnings goals they have in mind when there is high demand for cars. So the company communicated to drivers that they are not far from achieving their income targets when it was most beneficial for the ride-hailing firm to have more cars on the road. The AI technology makes it possible to collect data and lure individuals to take actions they would not otherwise opt for in order to advance the corporate objective. In effect, any firm can pretty much deploy information asymmetries to drive its own agenda unbeknown to its workers. Firms will need to make their own decisions as to what uses data and technologies are put to, but it is essential that finance leaders are aware of how data are deployed, as this can have wider consequences.

DIGITALIZATION MAKES ALL ENTERPRISES UNLIKE

As we go forward, digitalizing organizations understand that performance management has to become "more data-driven, more flexible, more continuous, and more development-oriented."[7] It is not just a matter of changing metrics or technical aspects of performance evaluation mechanisms. It is that there is a need to change who gives feedback, when it is given and the manner in which it is given. In addition, once feedback is received, the way in which it must be acted upon also changes in digitalizing enterprises. The first thing to acknowledge about all financial and accounting techniques is that their operationalization in organizations has always been highly context dependent. This is the case across enterprises, industrial sectors, and geographical locations. Everything we know about the use of management controls in decision-making of any sort points to techniques that are generic becoming ensconced in highly particular ways within enterprises. Financial practices gain technical traction with a high level of specificity. Organizations may be alike in their financial reporting, but they are always unlike in the ways they use and interpret accounting and other information types, and they retain distinctiveness that lends them strategic competitiveness. In both traditional industrial enterprises as well as cutting-edge digitally transformed enterprises, it is unlikely that this will ever change. The particular ways in which organizations operate will always remain particular!

As far as performance management systems go, their specific workings will remain individualized and customized. But digital for an enterprise means also that some important changes take place in parallel across all its units. The extent of impact on operations and the products, markets, and customer responses, as well as the timing of these effects to play out and the information tied to the consequences of action all vary. As tight dividing lines between strategic maneuvers and operational activities crumble in digitalizing organizations, performance evaluation becomes directed toward continuous, multifaceted and more comprehensive control actions. Feedback becomes ongoing, and is drawn from a variety of places and sources. So outcomes based on data analysis that takes place along ongoing time frames, whether categorized distinctly as strategic or operational, or as a *"strat-perational"* blend, also must be evaluated on a real-time continuous basis. The conventional approach to internal financial report production on a periodic daily, quarterly, or annual basis makes much less sense in a digital enterprise that reacts on the go.

ON BEING DATA-CENTRIC AND INTUITIVE

Some digital firms take the view that their performance management should rely less on subjective opinion, personal observations, and interpretations as well as intuition. Primacy is given to data that gets generated more and more from apps, platforms, and digital tools and observable formal evidential data. Other enterprises will more intentionally take account of subjective evaluations to accompany interpretations of formalized data whether quantitative, qualitative, or financial in guiding actions to be taken. An element of judgment and perhaps even idiosyncratic assessment of situations is regarded in these firms to lend competitive distinctiveness, which also needs to be evaluated and possibly rewarded. Some firms will recognize that machines will be able to replace tasks that are routine, arithmetical, and associated with structured problem solving. Digital technologies like RPA systems can readily do such tasks but they cannot generally engage with nonroutine tasks and unstructured problem solving. Where they are performed by humans, performance measures could integrate these in assessments. For now, machines exhibit only very limited intuition, imagination or creativity, and show little judgment or capacity to be explorative. Performance results reflective of individuals displaying these characteristics while intelligently integrating them with machine-based outputs in decision-making will be positively viewed by performance measurement systems that are digitalization adept. And such systems will show high specificities reflective of their context. Just like organizations can be alike in their services but unlike in their internal processes, so this must also apply to their performance assessment approaches. Ultimately, all enterprises exercise some element of individuality, but manifest common ground with others also.

For IBM, the journey has been one that moves away from the traditional performance management approach of ratings and annual reviews where employees identify their targets and goals at the start of the year and at the end obtain feedback on the extent to which the goals were deemed to have been achieved. IBM began departing from this approach a few years ago by inviting over 360,000 of its employees to develop a new system of evaluation. The overwhelming difference relates to a movement away from assessment of goal attainment toward continual feedback relating to skill sets that employees work to improve. IBM workers from across levels co-created the new system to emphasize the continuous updating of skills as a primary element of performance evaluation. Like many other enterprises, IBM had a sense that it needed to move away from appraising employees for reward purposes toward professional development resting on feedback, mentoring and coaching, and performance improvement through skills development. In situations where work has changed such that teams get created, different reporting structures get implemented for specific projects sometimes on a temporary basis, and there is greater interdependency between workers. The model of one individual getting assessed by a superior annually was viewed as unworkable.

Hiring at IBM often takes place on the grounds that individuals offer the capacity to learn and adapt, rather than on the existence of specific skills that an individual might bring because skills have a fast shrinking half-life. Potential to learn trumps ready skills. There is a realization that knowledge grows much faster than any individual's ability to grasp what there is to know. Consequently, humility is growingly a part of good leadership style and should underpin performance management systems.

Listening to others is a valued characteristic. The capacity to learn and change is what is regarded as the pathway to ensuring corporate survival. Learning itself within modern enterprises has taken a turn. Reverse mentoring is becoming commonplace where more junior workers are paired with senior executives who can be exposed to and learn about novel tech trends and digital innovations. Indeed, seniors are taught to unlearn what they know by juniors. The result is informed particularism within firms using similar digital means of doing business.

PREDICTIVE PERFORMANCE MANAGEMENT

Decision makers in digitalizing organizations will make greater appeal to data across the range of activities they have to perform. It is inevitable that if operational and strategic decisions become co-mingled in the face of the growing real time availability of big data, then that same growth of data will need to be collected, organized, analyzed, and used in performance management activities. It must be recognized that the availability of big data does not imply that the same people use different data in making decisions. The deployment of big data is increasingly undertaken by teams of individuals who collectively interface with one another and make decisions that are grounded in teamwork and collaboration. How to extract and incentivize value coming out of interactions in the face of different individuals collaboratively engaging with the data is something that has not been resolved within most performance management systems. Consequently, "anticipating new opportunities matters more than summarizing past results."[8] Where executives use big data analysis to determine trends and to predict market changes on the go, performance management systems likewise move toward "feed forward" information rather than "feedback" mechanisms, as they have done in the past. What must be borne in mind is that performance is the ultimate objective rather than performance management. But activities, decisions, and operations have to be managed with the involvement of people. And so, performance management systems that look forward, rather than compare what should have been with what is driving enterprise performance, are essential and unless conventional systems adapt, they will not perform.

All companies seek today to be leaner, more customer centric, and to act with greater agility. Different companies achieve this in different ways, and typically the performance management system has to support the changes that are put to work. At General Electric, the mechanism through which this is being achieved is a pro-development process where employees are given insights and nudged toward considering changing the ways they perform certain activities, or behaviors or practices. The performance evaluation system simply collects data and after processing makes suggestions to employees rather than being directive. The employee is co-opted into thinking through their personal growth in a manner that also takes account of enterprise environment changes. Other companies recognize that they have to adjust their performance evaluation systems to the demographics of their workforce, so for instance, a workforce of mainly millennials can have the organization choosing to conduct weekly performance feedback sessions as opposed to the more formal yearly performance appraisals favored in past times. Additionally, millennials and particularly Gen Zers prefer to take charge of their development and are perhaps more sensitive to negative feedback because they genuinely seek self-improvement and prefer to be self-critical based on evaluation information which they themselves assess and internalize. Consequently systems of self-review in terms of what workers seek rather than relative to external indicators of where they should be can be effective, especially where senior executives provide a motivational coaching role rather than an evaluative assessment.

Integrating data from a variety of sources is part of digitalizing firms which seek more predictive performance management orientations with statistical applications that assess vast amounts of data, identify patterns, trends, and data associations which are meaningful. These feed into what can be anticipated of a particular employee needing to address and assist in identifying for that worker the improvement in activities that are priorities, how that worker can better align operational activities with the broader direction the enterprise is taking, and even how performance measures ought to change as the environment alters and different metrics relevant to performance assessment come to light. Advances in predictive performance evaluation systems will likely go in the direction of information that can be accessed by different individuals working in teams or on projects, and as new data become uploaded, the interactions between these individuals and teams will alter the variables that will require continuous assessment. Perhaps deliverables will have to be altered frequently because variables that affect performance will emerge and will be dynamic. Feedback between actions and outcomes will feed new ways of envisioning what needs to be done.

HOW TO TRACK DIGITALIZATION

We have discussed how emerging technologies can digitalize certain processes. Examples are processing data, collecting data, and undertaking predictable physical work activities among many others. These activities have a high probability of being displaced by digital. People with skills in analytics, technology, and business will need to rethink how to configure automation so it produces growth and innovation. Tracking the speed, level, and extent of digitalization can be monitored as part of performance reviews. But it is likely to be the case that performance will increase as digitalization capacity is generated, and so what needs to be tracked is not only the impact and outcomes from digitalization but the measures that get created, too.

We have noted that the nature of the changing workforce implies expectations that deviate from those of more mature senior executives whose focus has, by force of habit, tended to be on outcomes rather than processes. Thus, performance management will need to move toward how quickly and effectively the workforce develops a knowledge base about digitization, machine learning, and AI, as these are important indicators of effectiveness. Applying an understanding of business cognizance, industry trends, and market needs, and coupling this with what digital innovations can do, will become important skill sets to develop, and will become key elements of performance indicators.

The COVID-19 pandemic has shown that people adapt to technologies quickly when essential, and can alter their workstyles and workspaces. The next decade will bring many more changes as rapidly as the pandemic did across enterprises. We know that growth of GDP per person across nations is forecasted to show a strong relationship with the proportion of existing work activities being displaced by automation. What this implies is that economic growth for most organizations will be closely associated with the rate at which their workforce skills and practices shift toward digital. Such change can be fostered in part through performance management changes. Organizations will need to become smart at monitoring training and reskilling and then aligning performance measures used before work structures were altered accordingly. Indicators will be needed to monitor the ability of the workforce to assess customer communications; engage in pilot tests for new work practices; test the effectiveness of virtual teams; grow capacity to adapt to continually altering conditions and markets; undertake iterations of activity programs; adhere to new forms of data exchanges; apply risk minimization measures; and comply with new standards and regulations. These are factors of digitalizing enterprises that might not have been priorities for more traditional firms. But as advances take place, novel measures will have to evolve in enterprise-specific ways to assess performance.

NOTES

1. Sirohi, Y. 2020. The importance of empathetic leadership in the age of disruption. CEO Insights. https://www.ceoinsightsindia.com/finance-leader-talks/the-importance-of-empathetic-leadership-in-the-age-of-disruption--nwid-2216.html

2. Kiron, D., and Spindel, B. 2019. Redefining performance management at DBS Bank. *MIT Sloan Management Review (March 26)*. https://sloanreview.mit.edu/case-study/redefining-performance-management-at-dbs-bank/

3. DBS Bank joins blockchain trade-finance network Contour. 2020. *The Straits Times* (May 11). https://www.straitstimes.com/business/banking/dbs-bank-joins-blockchain-trade-finance-network-contour#

4. Curzi, et al. 2019. Performance appraisal and innovative behavior in the digital era. *Frontiers in Psychology* (July 17). https://doi.org/10.3389/fpsyg.2019.01659

5. Schwarzmuller, et al. 2018. How does the digital transformation affect organizations? Key themes of change in work design and leadership. *Management Revue – Socio-Economic Studies* 29 (2): p. 114–138. https://www.nomos-elibrary.de/10.5771/0935-9915-2018-2-114/how-does-the-digital-transformation-affect-organizations-key-themes-of-change-in-work-design-and-leadership-volume-29-2018-issue-2

6. Crawford, et al. 2019. *AI Now 2019 Report*. https://ainowinstitute.org/AI_Now_2019_Report.html

7. Schrage, et al. 2019. Performance management's digital shift. *MIT Sloan Management Review* (February 26). https://sloanreview.mit.edu/projects/performance-managements-digital-shift/

8. Ibid.

CHAPTER **7**

Digitalization and Auditing

There are experts that are good in finance, and there are experts that are good in technology. To find an auditor that is good in both and understands the interdependencies is tough. But that is what we really need.[1]

—Isabel Witte, VP Finance and controller,
Siemens Healthcare

GL.ai is a technology capable of analyzing documents and preparing reports using reinforcement learning. The system was developed by PwC and a Silicon Valley company with an expertise in AI-enabled logic applications. GL.ai learns and becomes more capable with every audit. It has been trained on audit data from Canada, Germany, Sweden, and the United Kingdom. The way it works is to harness the firm's global knowledges and experience, which gets embedded into algorithms that replicate the thinking and decision-making of expert auditors. It will examine every uploaded transaction from users and find discrepancies, errors and possible fraud analyzing billions of data points in milliseconds. The system is being advanced and uses Natural Language Processing (NLP) to help make sense of complex lease agreements, revenue contracts, and board meeting minutes and to provide meaningful insights for clients. It sees what humans cannot and the more it's used – the smarter it gets! The technology is a prize-winning audit innovation – and fast learning to become better.[2]

Now is a time of significant change for audit assurance services. There exist many examples of assurance work that illustrate how digital technologies, such as blockchain platforms that can manage the integrity of data through value chains, are directly feeding into the auditor's function. In the past 10 years, new business models have emerged, automated technologies have advanced, and data availability has massively increased in volume and diversity. Audit professionals have much to ponder! Just over 60 years ago, auditing had to reinvent itself being faced with big growth in the range and volume of audit evidence to assess, and the complexities of business affairs rising rapidly. The need then was to maintain legitimacy and trust in audit engagements and to ensure the efficient use of resources and cost containment, which led to changes in how assurance was to be provided. Statistical sampling and the determination of confidence levels, alongside other mathematical techniques and metrics, were advanced to reduce audit evidence requirements while still retaining the legitimacy of audit work and ensuring client satisfaction. Innovations in business and the need for trust, especially in the light of many company failures following clean auditor reports and audit watchdogs tightening standards, have continued to concern providers of audit services. But new issues have additionally emerged. Not only are digital technologies leading to processes being standardized so data can move across systems and be manipulated more flexibly, but automation is affecting the quality of audit evidence and output, too. Auditors are entering environments that deploy new technologies but, additionally, these very technologies are altering the nature of audit work itself. It has become unviable for auditors to ignore the power of new technologies such as blockchain, RPA systems, AI systems, and machine learning, and ways in which cloud technologies and smart contracts used within firms are altering what is at stake for assurance work, as well as the manner in which audits are to be carried out.

This chapter discusses how digital technologies are affecting auditing, including big data analytics, robotic process automation systems (RPAs), AI systems, and blockchain. We also look at some security issues that auditors will need to understand and discuss the risks to auditing as a profession.

BIG DATA: BIG AUDIT QUESTIONS

For a long time, audit assignments have been assessed in terms of the sources of information required to be collected, organized, formatted, prepared, analyzed, and assessed to establish the length and the parameters of the engagement. Auditing has been premised on routine tasks being undertaken, often accompanied by extensive manual input. New technologies and data analytic tools are, however, now forcing re-evaluations of what constitutes effectiveness of audit work, and also raising the prospect of total population verifications. Carrying out tests on small samples of populations of transactions as part of the audit process, has in some situations been abandoned. What is becoming evident is that auditing standards are starting to lag behind some changes brought about by digital technologies.

There exists minimal guidance on when 100% testing is better than the selection of specific items for audit evidence. Sampling, of course, is not to be favored if there is significant perceived risk, or key items exist that ought to be examined, or if the population is small and heterogeneous. Cost and time are always issues the auditor must grapple with vis-a-vis sampling, and 100% testing to minimize risk through automated technologies enables total oversight at lower expense in many cases. In this sense, data availability, data analysis techniques, the growth of automated technologies, and the need for more reliable assessments are reshaping audit work, processes, and objectives. We'll see here that, broadly speaking, digital technologies enable full audits to be carried out via total accounting population assessments, which also widen the scope of work and recommendations auditors can offer their clients.

The AICPA's Accounting Standards Board allows for the deployment of business data analytics but the more difficult questions relate to whether it is financially and operationally viable to use big data analysis as part of audits. From a business perspective, audit work is highly competitive, and professional auditors may find it challenging to consider big data and automation issues because of the resource implications. Unless the payoffs are clear, movement will be slow. Conversely, if both economies and quality of audit outcomes can be improved, then big data analytics will progress in audit situations.

Most technologies face similar hurdles initially where costs do not justify altering mechanisms of business engagement, but as efficiencies kick in and technological adeptness rises, innovations gain traction. In a climate of growing data, it would be odd for auditors not to assess evidence that could influence their judgments.

Much that has been reported about the extent of the exponential rise of data we're witnessing is astounding. Of course, while the volume of data has grown this has been accompanied by a rise in the variety of forms of data, too. The velocity of data flows has likewise increased. A sea of data currently exists, and its diversity, size, and pace of growth is reaching ever new levels. Before digital, auditors focused on small population samples to make inferences since assessing the whole universe of transactional information would have been excessively time and resource consuming. Now that data volume, variety, and velocity are reaching new peaks, how audit work must react is essential to ponder. What must be understood is that traditionally, organizational data sources were collected with predefined purposes. They had specific intents in relation to information systems that were built around the needs to their users. Spreadsheets, records, and ledgers were designed to serve preset goals. Today, the overwhelming proportion of information is incidental to what organizations do. The data enterprises produce provide insight and hold much value even though most were not processed by the predesigned information systems that companies have traditionally installed. Today, *exhaust data* reflective of activities connected to the business, but not directly linked to economic exchanges, has become core to what enables certain organizations to stay viable. Texts, numbers, videos, pictures, audios, and other media formats existing in unstructured forms can prove highly valuable, not just to firms that will process such data for business intelligence but also in providing audit insights. Likewise, aerial views, drone videos, satellite pictures, and sensor signals are all being considered as part of audit evidence. Non-accounting data, when combined with business transactions data, no doubt enable fuller audits and reduce the possibility of bias. Big data, in other words, can enhance audit comprehensiveness and therefore lend trust and legitimacy.

One question that arises is, how far should the analysis of unstructured big data be part of audit work? And how should structured accounting data be meshed with unstructured non-accounting data to enhance audit value? Moreover, how far should auditors verify nontraditional data sources, and how should they aggregate different audit evidence types in ways that are methodologically rational and coherent? Further, how should the amount of audit evidence obtained from big data analytics be measured? These are issues that auditors are and will continue to face for some time. It may also be that standards of audit evidence themselves need to be re-evaluated in light of the availability of big data evidence. The emphasis on quality of evidence is important to assess, aside from the traditional quantity of audit evidence deemed to suffice. Questions about costs and benefits of different data analyses – as well as issues of relevance, reliability, and appropriateness and opinion forming, among others – have to be posed in relation to big data's impact on audits.

RPAS, AI, AND AUDITS

Big data analytics is making inroads into enterprises with the mounting use of digital technologies such as RPA and AI systems that are adding to data size and possibilities. Audit tasks themselves are being impacted by digital innovations. Cloud-based accounting systems have led to more standardization and as a consequence data is simpler to manipulate, access, and analyze. RPAs can assist in standardizing where there are requirements to make workflows more rapid, and the need exists to eliminate manual access and undertake data conversions. In considering data sources, RPAs can enhance pattern identification, language recognition, and problem solving in detecting anomalies. The extraction of information of accounting essence from documents including minutes, internal analyses, contracts, and so on can feed into audit evidence. Naturally, the larger the volume of data powered through algorithms, the greater the learning, which ultimately makes automated processes superior to human audit inputs in many situations. While RPA technologies allow data to be drawn from systems where humans would have undertaken the collection, they can provide much greater accuracy, scalability, and continuity of task engagements. The output from RPAs can be fed into AI systems, which identify errors, anomalies, potential fraud, and questions for further assessment. RPAs facilitate analytics, and with AI, can help to comprehend and visualize entire data populations indicating associations, outlying points and anomalies so that risk areas can be understood and highlighted. This makes the auditor's tasks more relevant to a future outlook, and being forward-focused represents a shift away from the traditional backward orientation.

Deploying automated technologies in audit work requires the auditor to invest in understanding the bases on which such systems operate. The auditor must take responsibility for testing algorithms used in audit work. Where machine learning agents are used to mimic auditor tasks, the risk exists that the automated systems ground biases and errors made by humans. These must be extracted out of systems to ensure accuracy as well as adherence to external regulations, and the removal of partialities that machines can replicate and even magnify.

What is significantly different in the use of automated technology assisting auditing tasks is that assessments of data can go beyond evaluating traditional financial data. For instance, records that could inform the audit process may encompass emails, social media postings, telephone conversations, customer reviews, and supply chain information exchanges. Some of this information may exist in unstructured formats that can be assessed through deep learning analysis. Explorations and mining via automated content analyses are the essence of deep learning. Deep learning systems can enable content analysis of say, internal auditor comments, as well as those from analysts, bankers, internal managers, and so on, The frequency say of certain word usage – such as "possibly", "probably", "generally", "perhaps", "to a degree", which might signal that deception or concealment could be present – can be examined. Naturally, the technology can readily signal the need for more focused examinations and verification. Auditors stepping into the realm of more and more big data analysis are making significant forays. KPMG for example is assisting clients in gaining new insights from enterprise information extending the audit services it provides. As John Kelly, senior vice-president of Cognitive Solutions and IBM Research, notes: "Auditing and similar knowledge services are increasingly challenged with tackling immense volumes of unstructured data. Cognitive technologies such as Watson can transform how this data is understood and how critical decisions are made."[3]

Auditors have in a similar vein successfully applied machine learning to automatically code accounting entries, which can also aid with improved fraud detection. Machine learning tools now allow humans to analyze much larger numbers of contracts such as leases within shorter time frames than via manual review. EY reports that such AI tools can make it possible to review as much as 70–80% of simple lease contents and 40% for more complex leases electronically with the balance reviewed by a human.[4] AI can, of course, help analyze unstructured data such as social media posts, emails, and conference audio calls, which can also save the auditor much time. The scope is broadened where economic and physical information and other evidence types that are part of traditional auditing domains of analysis are complemented with data that is more narrative and sometimes highly unstructured.

Big data insights can help guide clients who may be focused on traditional sources of information and this increases the role of auditors in the services they are able to provide. There exists much evidence that big data analyses corroborate and confirm the conclusions reached through more conventional audit work. This does not make this innovation in audit redundant but on the contrary, raises possibilities for more cost effective audit practices and the likelihood that traditional audit evidence gathering can be substituted with big data analyses in some cases. Moreover, big data analysis can also aid in enabling remote auditing or the outsourcing of audit tasks.

Big data analysis and the deployment of digital technologies engages the auditor differently and thereby opens up challenges. Accountancy institutes are grappling with how to ensure that audit training covers the requisite knowledge base so that auditors have the appropriate level of expertise, analytical skills, and competencies. An important question is how data scientists should be engaged with auditors – as service providers or partners – and to what extent should auditors invest in data science training. Should data scientists assist auditors in planning the audit, selecting audit tools, assessing database structures and data fields as well as in data extraction, risk analysis, performance of tests, and so on? One issue relates to determining the materiality of audit evidence from big data and how to fit this into the requisites of audit standards. The use of automated technologies and 100% populations being audited should not be taken to imply that audit outcomes are anything but statements of opinion. While whole populations can be tested, the comprehensiveness of audit work will be widened but the audit end result itself will remain a judgment rather than confirmation of correctness and total assurance of representation. The data analyzed renders possible automated assessments and predictions, but cannot comprehensively confirm nonbias. Comfort as to the accuracy of financial statements is what is desired rather than absolute assurance. The presumption that automated systems engaging audits of total populations can provide anything more than reasonable assurance would be misplaced.

BLOCKCHAIN IS HERE

Auditors are charged with performing inquiries, analytical procedures, verification, and substantiation procedures. There is little here that would suggest that big data analyses and the utilization of digital systems to achieve this should prove problematic. The intent of any audit is to operationalize procedures in order to give comfort that financial statements are free from material misstatements. If a technology gives greater probability that material misstatements as a consequence of deliberate failure to record transactions or perhaps because of genuine errors are unlikely to occur, then such a system is likely to prove useful to auditors.

Irrespective of the technology they use, auditors will consider data as part of the audit job to verify financial transactions undertaken with the inclusion of extensive third-party organization receipts (see Figure 7.1). Investors and external financial statement users

Figure 7.1 Conventional audit evidence.

desire reliable data as this increases the viability of making decisions based on financial reports. That confidence in the reliability of reporting is crucial. Auditors play a key role in this but must balance the level of tasks having to be undertaken as data grows and business becomes more complex; and if less resources are required to be spent on checking and verification while increasing the reliability and accuracy of the information reported, then this will be of benefit to their function. To this end, distributed ledger technology or blockchain systems are becoming part of the audit process. The mechanics though are different from conventional audit functions.

As we've discussed in Chapter 2, blockchains are databases that store data about transactions in a decentralized system. The data stored is accessible by nodes or members of the system. As blocks on transactions are generated they build the blockchain. Changes to a blockchain cannot be made, given the decentralized validation requirement that lends a high degree of transparency and assurance of nontampering. When a blockchain transaction is recorded, it gets authenticated. Say an organization obtains goods following the payment of an invoice, the blockchain will approve the invoice and verification of the information is undertaken. This would be confirmed through a hash where the information becomes encrypted within the record. So both parties have the authentication and there cannot be a ready possibility of any manipulation of the invoice data. Ordinarily, third parties with no interest in biasing information enable information verification by auditors. The blockchain system acts in a sense as that third party by virtue of the system's immutability (see Figure 7.2). Some audit work is undertaken conventionally without third-party verification where tracing of information takes place. The extension of blockchains in these areas further strengthens the quality of audits.

Many enterprises deploy blockchain systems. Banco Santander installed the first global blockchain-led money transfer service "Santander One Pay FX," which allows customers to make same-day or next-day international money transfers. It managed to reduce the number of intermediaries ordinarily required in such transactions increasing the efficiency of the process. IBM is experimenting with a World Wire payment network and Fidelity is using blockchains for custodial services. Citibank and Nasdaq also use blockchains to

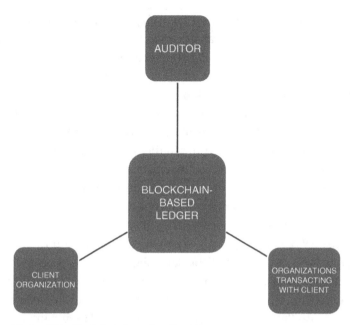

Figure 7.2 Blockchain-based audit evidence.

automate payment processing. Barclays is engaging in blockchain initiatives to track financial transactions, compliance, and fraud. It regards the technology as a new operating system "for the planet" while JP Morgan has a patent filing for applying distributed ledger technology for settling transactions between banks. The shipping line Maersk has put together a blockchain system to digitalize its entire processes across nodes. This is advancing toward the availability of real-time information to insurers and insurees with respect to ship location, condition, load, safety hazards, and so on, whereby say a ship enters a high-risk area, the system would detect its location and build this into insurance calculations. Walmart in a coalition with Nestle, Unilever, and Dole has placed its fresh food suppliers on a blockchain-enabled system.

The impact blockchains can have in some contexts is similar to what internet business models did to conventional industry players. For instance, platforms such as Skyscanner and Expedia have upended much of the traditional travel agency industry. Blockchain can remove the need for an intermediary like Expedia! TUI Groups and hotel aggregators such as GOeureka deploy blockchain systems to cut costs and increase transparency by directly giving customers access to hundreds of thousands of hotel accommodations. The power of blockchains thus extends to enabling novel business models which auditors are becoming exposed to.

Where blockchains affect business models, they make it unviable for auditors not to understand the implications of the technology in audit processes. EY is a forerunner in the use of blockchain technology in carrying out audit work. EY's "Blockchain Analyzer" initially offered its services to cryptocurrency companies allowing the gathering of an organization's total transaction data from multiple blockchain ledgers. So where a company uses currencies such as Bitcoin, Ethereum, or LiteCoin, EY obtains the data and can analyze transactions. The tool is highly useful in interrogating the data, performing analyzes of transactions, doing reconciliations and in identifying transaction outliers. But then a question to ask is, are cryptocurrencies cash or financial instruments? As Boillet[5] explains "new digital assets and their pace of change mean we must actively engage in developing new methodologies and tools" and she notes that cash is expected to be used as a medium of exchange, and as the monetary unit in pricing goods or services it should be used to such an extent that it would be the basis on which all transactions are measured and recognized in financial statements. Cryptocurrencies do not satisfy the definition International Financial Reporting Standards have provided. So then we might consider IAS 32's definition of a financial asset. This means any asset that is: (a) cash; (b) an equity instrument of another entity; (c) a contractual right to receive cash or another financial asset from another entity; (d) a contractual right to exchange financial assets or financial liabilities with another entity under particular conditions; or (e) a particular contract that will or may be settled in the entity's own equity instruments. So cryptocurrencies do not fit this bill either. They, in fact, come closest to being intangible assets (under IAS 38). That is, they give rise to future economic benefit, lack physical substance, are identifiable, controlled by the entity, and are not in scope of other standards. Going from here, the auditor would have to learn about the nature of the digital assets and their underlying protocols, as this is vital in assessing evidence from the blockchain. Intangible assets pose risks and therefore the auditor must ask for instance, whether the blockchain is widely used; if it is open source and the number of developers that use it; and, whether smart contracts execute automatic transactions and the risks this may raise. While blockchain technology presents challenges, EY continues to develop its application in auditing and tax work as well as in helping firms conduct business on public and private blockchains. EY uses its blockchain platforms to assist in the tracking of assets along complex value chains such as chicken and chicken products, and animal vaccines. It can even help its clients track wine with its Tattoo platform so the quality, provenance, and authenticity of imported European wines can be assured.

Some benefits of blockchains to the auditing task may not be apparent at first. While blockchain can reduce human input for repetitive tasks where the risk of error is very high, the automation of accounting functions really pays off. Efficiency also is enhanced because, relative to legacy accounting software, robustness of the system, and speed of data access increase. All this naturally translates into reduced audit costs. This form of cost containment should be taken into account when considering the adoption costs of blockchain technology implementation. But it is important to recognize some of the costs of using blockchains relative to the tangible benefits. Using blockchain does not make audit evidence error free or devoid of fraud. The perception of immutability should not imply total assurance. Moreover, the presumed reliability of blockchains can get organizations to put down their guards. This would be a mistake. And in this light, auditors have a duty of care to undertake proper assessments during audit work, which can extend also into advisory inputs to businesses using blockchain technologies as part of their digital transformation drive. The deployment of blockchains, especially where extensive transactions and interlinkages exist between organizations, requires the existence of consensus around standards adopted. This may entail much negotiation, and will be reflective of many factors, including complexities of the business, size of transactions, and competitive factors among others. Not all parties will want to make the investments involved.

It has been suggested that given that external auditors provide judgments on financial statements, on the surface, blockchains might be seen as having the capacity to disintermediate their role. Since a blockchain that is public is decentralized in its validation, that is, it is observable by all, the function and raison d'être of auditors could be questioned. It certainly is the case that the potential exists for block-chain technologies to lead to fewer audits given the traceability of more and more records in blocks. Automation through smart con-tracts implies automation of many audit procedures. But the rele-vance of auditors and the essence of audits in fact remain even in highly blockchained environments for several reasons. While the requirement to undertake reconciliations of many disparate data-bases is removed by blockchains given the demonstrable audit trail and immutability of records, the shifts blockchains can instill on audits enhance the potential for full and comprehensive audits that are con-tinuous. A blockchain is capable of recording authorizations and sup-porting documentation, integrating journals entries, and undertaking value transfers for transacting parties all on one platform. This opens the door to seeing transactions themselves as integrating records of the internal control and audit function! This is because confirmations and/ or reconciliations take place as transactions take place. The mirroring of exchanges in conventional double entries that focused on achieving retrospective forensic aims with a time lag can through blockchains become real time and simultaneous. The auditor is key in assisting enterprises to move in the transformation toward real-time auditing and reporting. Blockchains thus offer the possibility for auditors to move from a focus on transactional repetitive task engagements and compliance work toward greater provision of judgmental insights and client advisory services.

Even in the presence of advanced blockchain implementation, information serving as accounting input will need to be interpreted and categorized accurately prior to entry into the system. It will be the accountant's job to do this, as well as implement and maintain the system. Also monitoring payment contracts for goods and services, overseeing costs and income, tracking accounts receivables will for now be done principally by accountants and bookkeepers. Blockchain-based digital ledgers provide windows on transactions in a distributed manner, thereby embedding audit trails and extinguishing the require-ment to have reconciliations of database records. Smart contracts can hugely reduce reconciliation tasks. The underlying entries of transactions that are immutable capture also what an audit seeks to do but like test outputs, the auditors' assurance of reliability and perspective on the significance of the output is still required.

So in assessing the data reliability of a blockchain, there has to be an evaluation of how far the system can be altered or manipulated. Blockchain systems adopt a consensus mechanism to determine how agreements are reached between transacting parties before adding blocks. It is the auditor's role to assess the data reliability of the blockchain and whether the system is vulnerable to attacks. As an auditor evaluates a blockchain's data reliability, there have to be tests carried out on the susceptibility of the consensus algorithm to be compromised. Assessments should be made of the possibility of unauthorized transactions that are added to the blockchain. One conventional fraud situation auditors encounter conventionally is an expense taking place twice but being single counted. Similarly, a double spend can occur in a weak blockchain situation which must be tested for. Judgment and comprehension of accounting techniques and policy detail further make human input essential. Skilled audit professionals have to render legitimate judgments and apply insight in relation to findings since knowledge of standards, guidelines, and regulations remain requirements. In this sense, as we've seen before, for technology to offer value, technology by itself is insufficient. Human engagement must complement the technology being adopted.

In their current form, blockchain systems can be costly to adopt and the expenses stemming from data storage capacity can be high. The technology resources required, costs of implementation, investments in standardization, and skills acquisition are all factors that act as hurdles to blockchain adoption. Data privacy, as well as regulatory and security issues add to the concerns. This is the case for firms adopting the technology as well as auditors. However, the Big Four all have moved in the direction of blockchain adoption. Blockchains generally offer more security and are likely to find more usage as regulatory demands rise and agencies and authorities recognize their benefits.

Finance leaders, accountants, and auditors are recognizing the value of blockchain systems. Discernible trends already suggest the capability of moving toward automated processes which will influence audit processes. Audit work will inevitably alter, becoming in part substituted by automated processes but the technology will also partially supplement and augment it. This does not mean the end of periodic reviews and the requirement to assess automated accounting reports, but a different mind-set and training will have to exist. Auditors will be more deeply involved with the interface of business activities, automated technologies, and financial transactions, and their role in accounting reporting and assurance provision will enable them to extend the advisory functions and services they render. Further, the potential of continuous reporting will transform information readers' expectations and their interpretations of reports obtained. Reliance on financial information will remain and likely grow in many domains where fast decisions have to be made. As accounting reporting becomes increasingly continuous, the relevance of effective ongoing audits will grow also. The auditor's role will change, but it will not be eliminated.

NOTES

1. KPMG. 2017. Digital transformation: How advanced technologies are impacting financial reporting and auditing. https://home.kpmg/content/dam/kpmg/us/pdf/2018/02/us-jnet-2018-issue1-2-KPMG-Forbes-Digital-Transformation-report.PDF

2. Needham, L. 2017. Harnessing the power of AI to transform the detection of fraud and error. PwC (October 14). https://www.pwc.com/gx/en/about/stories-from-across-the-world/harnessing-the-power-of-ai-to-transform-the-detection-of-fraud-and-error.html

3. Faggella, D. 2020. AI in the Accounting Big Four - Comparing Deloitte, PwC, KPMG, and EY. *Emerj* (April 3). https://emerj.com/ai-sector-overviews/ai-in-the-accounting-big-four-comparing-deloitte-pwc-kpmg-and-ey/

4. Ibid.

5. Boillet, J. 2020. How to audit the next generation of digital assets. EY (January 30).https://www.ey.com/en_gl/assurance/how-to-audit-the-next-generation-of-digital-assets

CHAPTER **8**

Better Change
Your Mind

If you're an analog business, you have to reposition yourself rapidly. You have to blow things up . . . if you don't change your organization, it's going to change for you – it's going to be out of your hands.[1]

—Sir Martin Sorrell, founder of WPP and CEO of S4

Ping An Bank learned much about what could be done with digital at the time of the COVID-19 pandemic. Before the pandemic it had started a drive to transform its structure from the traditional hierarchical pyramid to a dumbbell-shaped organization where it increased the number of senior executives focused on digital transformation and IT. It kept the number of middle-level managers level in the face of growth and extended the scale of front-line market-facing teams.[2] Ping An Bank then introduced the Do It At Home campaign, offering contactless and smart services in its anti-coronavirus initiative. This allowed customers to undertake a variety of financial services on the Ping An Pocket Bank app. The app could be used for basic banking transactions, wealth management, insurance, foreign exchange, private bank or family trust, investor education, and more. Artificial intelligence–powered customer service provided 24/7 consultations. Customers learned quickly. Within two weeks, over 11 million transactions were carried out by more than 3 million customers with 475,000 customers viewing online lectures on mutual funds, PE investment, and financial laws and taxation.[3] Users of the app now exceed 100 million. To optimize its internal operations, Ping An Bank continues to drive technology projects like smart finance, smart risk management, smart operations, and smart marketing. The object is to support decision-making and management capabilities by replacing experience-driven operations with data-driven ones. And as Xie Yonglin, president and co-CEO of Ping An Group, notes: "We're hoping to make continuous breakthroughs in digitalization to set a successful example for China and the world's banking industry."[4]

In the 1980s, experts saw accounting as being in big trouble! The concern then was that the field lagged behind business, which was seeing the adoption of flexible organizational technologies such as just in time systems, quality costing, CAD/CAM systems, computer integrated manufacturing, and robots among other advances impacting firms across every industrial sector. Cost management and financial control techniques had not altered to support these hardware-based and production process focused innovations. Albeit with a lag, new financial control techniques were developed including throughput accounting, activity-based costing, target cost management, backflush accounting, balanced scorecards, and strategic cost analysis.[5] The problem was that accounting approaches had trailed organizational changes, consequently leading to weak business decisions, reduced competitiveness, and markets being lost. To many, accounting was the enemy of enterprise management. In fact, the enemy was that accountancy training fell short of what managers needed to maneuver and steer enterprises more effectively in the face of change. The issue of finance professionals having the right knowledge base to deal with changes in business environments and the accelerating advent of digital technologies is once again forcing accountancy and finance functions to ponder ways of maintaining relevance. But the problem this time is of a different form, depth, and magnitude.

To grasp how digital technologies can enhance finance's role in management, it's important to recognize that most changes are now software-based and are reshaping not just operations but also the decisions that impact operations. As Marc Andreessen, founder of Netscape, Opsware, and Andreessen Horowitz notes: "Software is eating the world." The power of data arises from being able to guide decision makers to act intelligently – but this only comes about if the data judiciously embeds sufficient usefulness. This is unachievable if accounting training, expertise, and knowledge do not align with data's new realities. No doubt, executives should continue to pursue organizational performance growth, cost containment, optimized operational activities, and increased revenues. These are conventional objectives for most enterprises and must remain. CFOs are recognizing, however, that a new perspective on financial intelligence to aid managerial decision-making in digitally transforming environments has become essential and a time lag in doing so is unaffordable. Technologies that in past decades enabled greater production flexibility, volume increases, and product diversity and sophistication to the ones today that alter the vocabulary, language, and premise on which decisions and actions are made, present the most significant challenge that finance leaders have ever had to face.

Accounting information and guidance that aids improved service, greater agility, and enhanced competitiveness is ultimately what finance teams are there for. For this, they must come to understand how digital technologies enable decisions, processes, and organizational objectives to be determined and met. They must be able to give guidance on potential business advances and novel value-creation pathways to pursue. Understanding digital technologies, and how they change the financial circuitry and DNA of decision-making is key. We've noted earlier that accountants have always been smart at producing decision-making information but that they need to get smarter by adopting a different accounting worldview. Take, for instance, their recognition that implementing bots and adopting RPA technologies can increase volume throughput multiple folds with very minimal outlay. This is self-evident. Going further, accountants also are seeing that the deployment of machine learning and AI, where certain actions can be driven through automation, represents a step change in how enterprises function, can gain speed, volume, accuracy, and increase the effectiveness of actions. So what else must be understood?

This chapter explores what is now required of finance professionals. It discusses how past conceptions of management are more harmful than useful for aiding the finance function deliver value. A discussion of novel skill sets that are part of digitalizing firms points to the changes in expertise that finance professionals must be open to. The chapter then considers risk issues, the need for caution with data, and the importance of navigating enterprises without seeking normality in digital because the consequences of not doing this will stop growth.

UNITE AND CONQUER: THE NEW DATA MANTRA

Investments that are regarded as strategic in digital do not totally conform with the assumptions of past business understandings. Likewise, costs and revenue sources, and expenses and expenditures, as noted in earlier chapters, have also developed different relationships in the digital world, which has implications for how they should alter decision-making. Additionally, we have seen that fixed costs can often be *variabalized* and variable costs can be made fixed in digitalized contexts. It turns out that operational and strategic action, costs and revenues, and fixed and variable costs all reveal more interweaved relationships in digital. These changes need to be picked up by accounting information to usefully guide how decisions can drive increased enterprise value. This may not be easy for accountants.

Strategy has, for many decades, been the subject of intense reflection by management theorists and business leaders. Not all agree on a definitive conception of strategy. Some view it as the determination of a scope and direction for an enterprise over the long term and the manner in which resources ought to be configured so that stakeholder and market needs are fulfilled. Others suggest that it is about the desire to assess the present and anticipate market and industry changes to bring about a successful future. Strategy has also been viewed as emerging over time as intentions collide with and accommodate a changing reality. Strategy has conventionally been the basis for defining operations, with wider business and environmental factors speaking to strategy reformulation. If we regard strategy as a frame of reference that tells us the decisions we need to make to pursue business activities, and think of these decisions as having to occur continuously so that they encompass marketing maneuvers, investment identification, branding efforts and so on, then operations should, by essence, support strategic action. In the context of digital transformation, old industrial worldviews about strategy limit the role of data. As Dan Schulman, CEO of PayPal, notes: "The biggest impediment to a company's future success is its past success." This was noted in chapter 6 but we need to look at this more deeply.

The problem is that strategic intent presumes that protracted time periods are required for an organization to define, and when necessary, to alter its directional purpose. But if the capacity exists to rethink alternative courses of action continuously then accountants cannot adhere to a pre-digital visualization of their function. Strategy and operations intermesh in digital – the process of data capture,

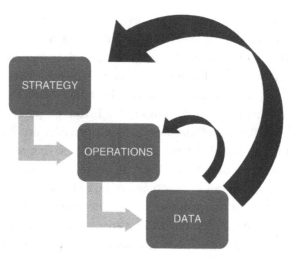

Figure 8.1   Refining operations and redefining strategy.

decision-making, and action becomes, "strat-perational" so to speak. In digital, strategy is the here and now, telling us whether our operations need refining and our strategic intents need redefining (see Figure 8.1). This means that accountants cannot lock in conventional rationales into new digital technologies whose information potential, stemming from operations to alter strategy, is immense. Indeed, accounting processes by virtue of digital technologies, enable finance to play an implicit strategic function.

Letting go of kneejerk presumptions that short-term actions should be well differentiated from long-term aims is a challenge for any executive. After all, intelligent business school professors have long held that management controls must keep the strategic apart from the operational. So it'll be difficult to accept that we should now favour keeping operational data much more deeply integrated with strategic intelligence and rethinking. But in digital, the short term and the long term are more closely coupled than in conventional industrial businesses. A decision to pivot an initiative in a certain direction creates data that get analyzed in real time. Aggregate data translate into information that feeds into further decision-making about the next move or sets of actions. Broad business goals get pursued with continuous realignment. At times, there is enough information from the data obtained to steer the business into entirely novel areas of activity. The broad business hypothesis being pursued may alter as a result of assessing information from operational decisions. No small sets of data can be islands dissociated from impacting wider organizational agendas. Managing in real time and quantifying short-term returns is as important as it always has been, but this must now recognize that longer-term changes share dependencies with these ground level operational activities. The interplay between action and pivoting of the business must be continuous and flexible. What many business gurus refer to as agility in digitalizing enterprises is, in a sense, the rejection of a demarcation between operational activities and strategic moves. Digital transformation means the two are suffused and thus forcing a separation between them can be artificial, if not harmful. Indeed, it may even be a relic of status differences whose time has elapsed. Gen Zers will resist notions that intelligence from operational data cannot be compounded into something that has strategic significance, and rightly so. This is not to say strategy is dead. It just should not be distanced from real-time action as to preclude what can be drawn from short-term activities and operational on-goings feeding into it.

Accounting forces us, for good conventional external reporting reasons, to keep say current accounts distinct from longer-term accounting items. But in relation to management in digitalized contexts, the short term and the long term are in fact not very far apart, as real-time data analysis links in to an enterprise's broader directional trajectory. Let's take an example: Capex is not the same as Opex to accountants. In assessing investment projects in digital, we should not import this differentiation. As we mentioned in Chapter 3, working out payback breakeven times, internal rates of return, and discounting projected cash flows, and so on proffer the allure of financial sophistication that conventionally has been prized. But, in fact, this likely ignores what is really of essence. The returns from production technology changes or investments in expansion have always been relatively easy to assess since the deliverables can be made to echo the objectives of the proposals. A digitalization initiative, however, may not meet the finance function's expectations that the project's payoffs must be earmarked at specific time points and that they can be assessed in relation to the outlay required. The project may be much more about creating valuable insights from data tied to its implementation. Chances are, the data generated will point to further digitalization moves that will trigger more data output for analysis. Competitive action may become more rapidly based on such data and feed into improving the customer experience, delivering products faster, strengthening market position, pointing to desirable marketing responses, pinpointing valuable price alterations, making the workforce more efficient, indicating useful product design changes, and so on. It would be difficult, if not disingenuous, to look at a digitalization proposal in terms of cash flows generated, fixed investment outlays, servicing cost requirements, and working out payoffs, and try to feed all this information a priori into investment appraisal scenarios that objectively link time to returns in terms of ROI, net present values, and internal rates of returns.

While digital may not conform to past financial management edicts, the evidence shows that high financial yields can be had from digitalization projects. One study reports that 60% of enterprises engaging in a digital transformation investment end up with novel business models, and for those firms that gross over US$1 billion a year, another US$700 million is generated within three years.[6] Most of the benefits arise from improved operational efficiency, faster time to market, and better met customer expectation. Such outcomes do not accrue because predetermined timelines were fixated on nor can they be ascribed as identifiable income payoffs that align closely with payment sequence predictions made at the outset. The overall returns can be sizable but digitalization investment proposals tend not to pass muster unless accountants, as information gatherers and reporters, understand and make visible the power of digital transformations without the imposition of conventional control hurdles.

Investments into new digital technologies such as RPAs, machine learning, and AI, as well as facilitating advanced analytics, can – within the finance function itself – bring huge benefits. They can enable a movement away from a transaction focus toward providing more extensive and deeper insights to decision makers. Finance professionals must not only revise how they approach investment decisions from other organizational units but also look at assessing the digital investment potential flexibly within their own finance function processes. They must facilitate evaluations of initiatives and proposals from finance managers using the same widened lens they apply more generally to gauge digital investment impacts on agility and organizational effectiveness.

It is probably less and less true that what does not get counted doesn't count for much in decisions taken. Still, where counting matters a great deal, accountants must make sure to count what has not in the past been counted. In considering digitalization opportunities in finance or in other parts of the organization, finance teams have to show flexibility by not invoking understandings of business fundamentals that are no longer in play. Creating a different future is not easy when you do not know how to visualize it, but gauging the continued usefulness of mechanisms in new contexts has to be a first step.

WHAT SKILLS?

In assessing the potential of digitalization investments, accountants must also take note of other digital business realities. We have discussed network effects, subcost pricing for market leadership, and data production, process, and customer knowledge from big data, and so on, suggesting that firms that effectively utilize digital technologies can get larger, which enhances their data growth, enabling further growth. As digital enterprise markets evolve, large players get larger and less customer footfall remains for smaller incumbents. A near "winner-takes-all" situation can arise in some industries. Of importance is that the generation of data, which through resulting actions, spurs more data as part of the business model, can be a valuable competitive force enabling extreme growth. This concept has not been part of conventional business logic. The new logic is important for accountants to learn, as they'll need this to alter the ways they serve other parts of the enterprises. A technology-focused finance function demands new skill sets and competencies to move the digital transformation agenda forward.

A Grant Thornton study[7] suggests that finance chiefs will need to adjust their recruitment and retention strategy to manage the human versus machine relationship. Half of the finance executives surveyed believe that technology advances are impacting financial management and that finance team aptitudes are in need of change. The need to acquire an understanding of digital is not going unheeded by finance leaders. One study of accounting and financial professionals reveals that reskilling is a must, with 62% of respondents perceiving a "significant skills gap." Accountants regard artificial intelligence, cloud computing, and mobile technologies as being the most impactful on their work.[8] Another survey of finance professionals reports that training existing staff was the most critical investment required for driving increased productivity and growth where new technology is adopted and more data sources need to be looked at.[9] A large study of over 4000 accountancy and finance professionals from across 12 countries also reveals that over half believe digital skills to be "extremely relevant." Commenting on this, Helen Brand, the chief executive of the ACCA accountancy body that carried out the study notes: "To ensure that professional accountants are effective, they need to broaden their knowledge base from the application focus that they may traditionally have had, to the understanding of how technology and data create value for organizations."[10] The president of the Institute of Chartered Accountants in England and Wales (ICAEW), David Matthews, likewise speaks of the "potential power of data analysis and artificial intelligence,"[11] which is fundamentally changing the profession. Its chief executive, Michael Izza, sees the "unprecedented opportunities" that exist for businesses and accounting professionals.[12] This is echoed in a PwC study of 1,581 CEOs in 83 countries, which reveals that 75% of CEOs see their upskilling programs as having achieved greater innovation and accelerated digital transformation, helping to grow the business, improve talent acquisition and retention, and increase workforce productivity.[13] CPA Canada has also developed in a similar vein a data management certificate to help its members harness the power of data.

Based on extensive evidence, it is clear that both technical and softer skills are essential for finance executives in the face of the growth of advanced technologies, including particularly AI and machine learning.[14] One study reveals that the biggest impact on firm productivity where digitalization is taking place is from the upgrading of skills – both technical and managerial.[15] Skills such as communication, leadership, critical thinking, and collaboration, aside from technical knowledge, data analytics, and domain expertise are viewed as critical. Others see the primary need as being much more technical.[16] In relation to management accountants wishing to stay at the C-suite level, their competencies relating to business analytics as well as their statistical, mathematical, and programming skills to be able to effectively use AI and machine learning must be increased. In fact, the suggestion is for accountants to further their understanding of the following: statistics including linear and nonlinear methods and spline techniques, data mining, probability as well as mathematics including linear algebra and optimization; simple algorithms and their assumptions including nonparametric algorithms; resampling methods such as bootstrapping and cross-validation techniques; an AI/machine learning software package; a language such as Python or R; databases such as SQL and MySQL; and importantly the ability to understand and differentiate between causal and predictive analysis to provide more valuable business information to managers. Some highlight the importance of understanding the capabilities of software, data visualization, data warehouse management, basics of coding, and analysis skills among essential technical skill requisites.[17]

As machines take over repetitive mundane work and as many activities become hybrid human-robot tasks, both technical and social skills will be essential for accountants to invest in. The technical skills are important as accountants need to deal directly with machines or interface with people that do. But social skills are also of growing relevance, particularly as accountants become more involved in providing and interpreting information relating to business activities as opposed to focusing on financial statements. Social skills that are increasingly relevant include conflict solving, tolerance of uncertainty, innovation focus, and leadership skills. Different commentators have diverse views on the extent and types of technical expertise and social skills required of finance professionals, and it is likely that differing contexts will make different demands on skill sets. What is evident is that the work of accountants is changing, and their expertise must adapt. In a world of IoT, AI, and big data, the capacity to make real-time data-based decisions is crucial. But also, many avant-garde accountants are seeing themselves as business translators who can drive innovation and digitalization initiatives by bridging technical expertise with business needs. Those who adapt will retain and gain relevance.

RISKING DIGITAL

Risk management and understanding ethical issues are two important skills highlighted by both executives and commentators in relation to digital transformation requisites. Risk can entail corruption of data as well as fraud and manipulation which are as much a part of AI model operations as they are in conventional high human input situations. Accountants have over a long time frame inserted checks, balances, and forensic mechanisms of oversight to deal with erring human input. Algorithms have less well-developed systems of detection, yet their processing of data and decisions can be highly voluminous and introduce new complexities. Risks grow exponentially as the ubiquity of data extends. Various categories of risk have become relevant in digitalizing contexts, including cyber risk where clarity on risk appetite; protection and preservation of information assets; capability to respond to threats and incidents; and resilience are important factors. Fraud and security risks will engage the attention of finance professionals across more and more areas, including improper forecasting, fraudulent credentials, unrecorded transactions, fictitious disclosures, privacy breaches, and weak internal controls. AI and machine learning technologies naturally can analyze very large volumes of transactions with the capacity to detect complex patterns in real time, which enhances the potential isolating the source of errors and taking corrective action. Also, a key benefit is the minimization of false positives, which enhances the user experience and customer satisfaction, and naturally reduces costs and time resources.

Regulatory matters also have to be taken into account. Technologies often outpace the capacity of regulators to deal with their implications, and different industries and national contexts adopt differing views on regulatory mechanisms. Finance leaders have to stay ahead of regulations and compliance, and the implications of current and future regulations on data and information. Automated fraud detection systems can, to a degree, be linked to changes in rules, policies, and regulations, which can prove especially useful in modern digital banking contexts.[18] However, the consequences of using technologies can cause an enterprise to fall foul of regulations unwittingly. Accountants and auditors have successfully put to use applications that are proving helpful in conventional accounting work that used to require much human input. For instance, auditors use anomaly detection applications to detect possible accounting fraud (such as unusually large or repetitive items, several payments to one address, suspect invoices, etc.) by testing items such as journal entries to identify questionable deviations. All transactions are looked at to assess whether items have been inputted in error or something nefarious has taken place. Instead of applying conventional methods resting on random sampling to detect anomalies or unintentional errors, public accountants can assess all transactions, which lends greater legitimacy to the audit tasks. In a database of 50 million entries, three may be highlighted, enabling audit risks to be much reduced. The level of accuracy can be very high. For instance, EY's anomaly detection program, Helix GLAD, enjoys a 97% detection accuracy level.[19] Likewise, Accenture uses an anomaly detection solution for its expense reporting system to augment its rule-based analytics system. This has been successful in reducing inefficient audit time dealing with an excess of "false positives."[20] But it must be kept in mind that AI models naturally can learn from data, and in the process their logic changes when they are retrained to learn from novel data. Actions based on AI learning feedback loops must be monitored so that they remain within the confines of regulatory structures.

De-risking needs to be designed-in, especially since 24/7 continuous control is part of digitalized operations. In dealing with the ubiquity of data and its continuous formation, machine-formulated actions need to adhere to regulatory stipulations that themselves may be changing. AI recommendations may also develop inherent biases, which become systematized into decisions and actions, which then give rise to different risks across categories from compliance to data privacy to reputational, which need to be tracked. Data analytics can lead to iniquitous decisions for staff, customers, and other stakeholders. Different controls can be deployed to mitigate this risk. Considering the types of actions that could be affected from AI-based analytics is of first-order importance. Case sensitivity should delimit the extent of risk taking that a business unit might choose to accept. For instance, the chatbot a lender uses to signal the level of borrowing an individual may be extended or recommending that an investment trust may require tighter controls than other applications where outcome risk-iness is of a lower order. There may, in addition, be continuous reas-sessments of checks, limits, and interdiction on the usage of certain data. Assessing data source can also prevent the development of risks at later stages of analytics. Naturally, AI model development can avert certain emerging risks, so determining methodologies of analyses will be useful and should be understood by finance leaders.

Using externally developed applications poses the threat of import-ing risks. The majority of enterprises partner with third parties such as technology providers, service providers, consultancies, data labelers, and so on to develop and use AI and machine learning technologies, which introduces vulnerabilities into the complex AI supply chain. While accountants understand third-party risk, conventional software development differs because of the probabilistic and nondetermin-istic nature of AI. The key is for firms to build and deploy respon-sible AI systems from the get-go.[21] Overall risk should be preempted at the design and implementation phase of an AI system to reduce the chances that it performs illegal, unethical, or unintended operations. Companies will be held accountable for what their AI delivers, so it is best to take preventive measures.

AI solutions are a growing part of vendor-developed software, as well as hardware-and software-enabled services that a business may use. This can insert within the business new and unchecked risks.[22] A large retail enterprise operating in many international regions may install AI features from periodic updates produced by a vendor-based customer-relationship-management application. It could well be unaware that the updates raise new data-privacy and compliance risks in some but not all territories the firm operates in. The AI system should ground models that are consistent with the enterprise's risk appetite and values. Matching risks to returns is something finance professionals are good at doing. That expertise should extend to the installation of AI technologies within their firms.

There exist wider-level risks of industrial disruptions through novel technologies and platforms that create major business shifts. Finance professionals will need to understand the implications of the types of risks emerging as a result of digitalization advances. Emerg-ing technologies such as cloud, data analytics, and robotic process automation have become top cybersecurity investment priorities.[23] As digitalization and remote work accelerates, and lines among employees, customers, contractors, and partners/vendors are blurring, many traditional network perimeters and boundaries are becoming obscured. Users, workloads, data, networks, and devices are every-where, and a "zero trust" perspective is being adopted by enterprises to deal with the ubiquitous nature of these domains. Finance teams must be able to raise awareness on cybersecurity risks and best practices, and to provide frequent updates on compliance changes and needs.

No matter what risk management measures are taken, risks will remain and adverse consequences of failures will result. How much should the accountant allow for investing in information security? The Gordon–Loeb[24] model provides a good approach to determining this. These questions could be asked:

- How much is the data worth?
- How much is the data at risk?
- What is the data vulnerability – that is, what is the likelihood that an attack on the data could be successful?

Mathematically, the model shows that generally investing in infor-matics security should be limited to at most 37% of the predicted loss. So suppose the attack likelihood is 25%, and if an attack occurs it has a 60% chance of being successful then we need to look at the data value. Say this is $10 million; then the enterprise should at most invest $0.37 \times 0.25 \times 0.6 \times \$10,000,000 = \$555,000$ in security, including computer security and cybersecurity that encompasses the risk of data theft, loss, damage, or corruption. Such an investment does not likely generate profit so it is an investment into averting losses.

The finance function needs to assess the costs in relation to the payoffs from digitalization initiatives where data risks are present. The costs can be high but the market for cybersecurity is growing alongside the implementation of digital in businesses. In fact, digitalization goes hand in hand with security investments. One example is Wipro Ltd., a global information technology, consulting, and outsourcing company with headquarters in Bengaluru with sales exceeding $8.6 billion. The company supports firms with their digital transformation objectives

and packages cybersecurity measures to support digitalization investments. Its digital technology provision revenues comprise more than
40% of the company's total sales with a sizable portion tied to its
cybersecurity facilitation. Any digital investment must factor in the
diminution of vulnerability through systems choices so that data is
safeguarded and security breach cost impacts are taken into account.
This invites the finance professional to be current with technological choices and options. The Gordon–Loeb model is an established
and well-tested model with much empirical evidence of enabling
enterprises to deal with cybersecurity cost control.

In relation to skill sets, risk management in digital tech-heavy
enterprises requires finance professionals to understand in broad
terms the analytic techniques that are used and their risk implications,
including whether performance and interpretability of output need
to be assessed and monitored. Additionally, some understanding of
approaches to test for stability, bias, and response fairness is important. The ability to explain to executives the extent and nature of risks
embedded in a model is essential, based on a comprehension of data
features and changes in the technology with the possible attendant
risk consequences. Legality and compliance are issues that must concern finance leaders as much as profitability and ethical engagement.

THE HIDDEN SIDE OF DATA: CAREFUL!

Designing managerial aid mechanisms in enterprises can raise an
array of ethical challenges and the finance team has to be aware that
digital systems shape decisions and operations that do not exist in a
vacuum. Systems are never neutral or impartial – they affect social
outcomes and have behavioral consequences. Accounting systems
designed by finance professionals embed cultural values, understandings, worldviews, biases, and precepts that affect the direction taken
by those who use them. In the context of digital technologies and
particularly AI applications, human decisions and values get baked
into predictions and machine outcomes. A plethora of social complexities – including issues of power, fairness, interests, rights, markets,
liberties, bias, and so on – shape their output. Data processing culmi-
nates into outcomes that shape peoples' behavior. We already know

that poor use of mathematical modeling can lead to policy making that can cost lives.[25] AI applications reflect the decisions humans make and mirror the values they draw data from while their logics encompass the values of their designers. They cannot be objective since they are technologies that arise from the contexts they inhabit and become agents of economic and social changes which lead to their further build-up of logic.

This implies that finance leaders must be cognizant of ethical issues relating to the roles they play in the design, uses, and outcomes from the systems developed and deployed. While accounting and finance professionals cannot be expert ethicists, they need to be aware that there is a whole canon of evolving knowledge centered around AI ethics that concerns itself with wider social questions about the effects of AI systems and the choices made by their designers and users.[26] Of importance is for finance leaders to be aware that they should interrogate whether, when, and how machines should make decisions about human actions – and whose values should guide those decisions. This will raise questions to do with privacy, transparency, user consent, and so on, which go beyond the technical make up of digitalization initiatives.

It would be facile to think that data are data no matter what, but data are subjectively constructed representations. In analyzing data using AI systems, finance professionals have to recognize that unlike conventional rule-based programs, such models are statistical worldviews. They lead to responses based on machine learning that absorb a partial notion of what the data subsumes, and this may be imperfect. It would be okay if this could be checked readily, but the problem lies in the rapid scale-up of systems where errors become more and more deeply hidden. Many examples exist of chat boxes that deviate from accepted social norms in their output because they absorb biases from the data they draw on. In the public domain, these defects can be detected by interested parties. In commercial contexts, this is less likely to happen, and algorithms with errors can build up without correction for some time, which can lead to inappropriate outcomes.

What's more, insights from algorithms are extrapolations from the past, though some of that past may be very recent. Accounting reports especially to external parties have tended to be historical. The reliance on big data insights retains, at least in part, the historical gaze of accounting information. Although this is not necessarily a drawback as the implications derived from information are put to use to shape the future, a risk exists that the presumed verity of the information extends very wide because it draws on a large volume of data, structured, and unstructured, and it continuously benefits from being refined via machine learning. Overreliance on data-based insights can result from the perception that it is mathematical, empirical, and evidence-based, and therefore more sound than human compiled information reports. Executives can become less circumspect when the presumption of the data's objectivity is thought to be in place. The act of quantifying via algorithms or models provides executives an opportunity to outsource decision-making authority to number-based decision-making. As a consequence, key business decisions can become delegated to the purported neutrality of model generated numbers.[27]

Aside from being aware of this, accountants need to know too that say, a revenue forecast that is algorithmically derived, will integrate within it only a partial view of what can be analyzed and extrapolated. The wider fundamentals can be left out, and a decision maker's presumption that there is comprehensiveness of factor assessment can lead them to reduce their own judgmental input. Over time, this can result in a loss of critical understanding and logic checks. The introduction of bias as well as narrowness of assessment into AI systems output can be prevalent. Indeed, it can be to the extent that this becomes institutionalized. Numerification can change the nature of finance work and knowledge. That is not to be avoided necessarily if done intelligently, but falling prey to algorithmics and statistical rituals in an unthinking manner has made some disciplines poorer.[28] This cannot be allowed to happen to finance and accounting expertise. If the data incorporates bias, then machines will not remove the bias that is built in. As an example, data indicative of customers having certain preferences, will lead companies to pitch product and service offerings in a targeted manner. However, customers that are potential segments for service provision but about who there is no data history availability, will be left out. In this light, Barry Melancon, president and CEO of the American Institute of CPAs, notes that: "As we become more reliant on machines, we have an obligation to ensure the right inputs are being entered into these sophisticated systems and that outputs are being accurately assessed."[29] Wider insight not built into data cannot be had from algorithms. AI's focus is on calculative input from data embedding structured ways of solving problems. Of relevance to specific situations, however, will be tasks that require unstructured problem solving, nonroutine task engagement, creative insight, innovative input, improvisation, empathy, and political awareness of decision-making contexts among others. In a sense, the newness of digital ironically makes more pronounced the repetition of what has been done manually and structurally in the past. Savvy executives look beyond objectively derived signals seeking what also seems subjectively appropriate. Overreliance on ill-configured AI can lead to actions that put an enterprise on the road to irrelevance.

WHAT "NEW NORMAL"?

There is no "new normal." Automated technologies ensure business moves in novel directions at an accelerating pace. Insufficient time remains at any stop-off to grasp respite from change or to let normality embed. In digital, newness is a continual state that does not permit structures to form with permanency. Forging ahead is the only precept for digitally transformed enterprises. Not unlike continuous arbitraging, accounting has to be ceaseless in representing the state of play and point to avenues for action. Accounting in this sense, has to shift its narrative – it has to be about creating the future based on the present rather than only the past. If finance professionals do not recognize the size and speed of the digital juggernaut marching through business then they will lose the potential of transitioning to a novel role in capturing data, converting it to information and generating new knowledge that powers action and innovation. Finance will not just let go of the opportunity to evolve, but will also dissipate its hold on the reporting of economic transactions because such reporting is itself becoming integrated with other data forms that other information specialists can learn to deal with. Accounting language has to be suffused into broader data and information structures because this will happen with or without the finance function's involvement.

Figure 8.2 The traditional focus on linearity.

Up to now, accounting has come at the tail end of enterprise activities. Business thinkers have for decades believed that people charged with senior organizational responsibilities must develop strategies and make decisions about the broad direction their enterprise can take. The strategies that end up getting pursued, over time, get structured into procedures, standards, operating processes, budgets and so on. These structures then determine the information systems, including accounting applications, that then work on converting data into information that can be used by decision makers (see Figure 8.2). The accounting information assists managers to identify issues, take actions, and monitor outcomes. These actions may be operational or they may redirect the strategic intents of the organization. Within the confines of the linear relationship where strategy dictates structures in firms that then determine what accounting system have to do, accounting applications can be incrementally refined to match growing complexities in the business environment.

The "strategy-structure-accounting" direction of travel has been presumed to hold where broad plans determine the architecture of enterprises and the way they are to function with accounting information facilitating the process by which strategic intentions are implemented through operations. As we've seen in prior chapters, digital is splintering this linearity. Accounting has to become much more than a mirror of economic activities that get captured in P&Ls and balance sheets. The notion that strategies delimit firm structures which then dictate the evolution of accounting systems is quickly becoming a defunct conception of accounting's place in business. Where accounting embraces the capture of wider data forms from a diversity of new sources, heightened speed and greater depth, it moves the enterprise forward in parallel with changes in strategy and structures adopted. Persisting with the conventional idea that strategy, structure, and accounting must follow a slow and narrow logic of sequence is a relic of times past that will destroy business. If finance does not step up to digital, it will become Judas at the table and managerial trust will slip.

Aside from understanding that strategy-structure-accounting linearities no longer prevail, finance leaders have to know too ways in which human versus machine relationships are changing. They must also learn many aspects of how digital technologies work and understand that their work will change, and in particular that digital means there'll be a lot more insight driven analytics to steer organizations. Data analytics is among the most significant priority new skills for finance executives, and a key competence to be honed is how to make more of new insights that aid managerial decision-making. Additionally, understanding innovation, digital entrepreneurship, applications developments, digitized customer experience management, and the altered financial circuitry of digitized enterprises are all knowledge bases that finance leaders will not be able to do without. Accounting must, in other words, strengthen what it has been about, as well as undergo a transformational reconstitution of its own raison d'être. Accountants have never had to confront a disruption such as this but all the while, accounting must continue to rapidly become what it never was. The disruption is one that is epic and that demands of finance professionals the capability to rewrite the book by which they operate. Accountancy education and training have entered a new realm that is wider and technologically more demanding and that urgently requires sharp cogitation if the field is to retain its relevance going forward. Within companies, changes in the finance mind-set necessitate C-suite rethinking articulated and accepted from the top, because entry-level incumbents already understand that new skill sets are a requirement rather than an option.

The notion to be seized is not just that digital implies that accounting must catch up with technology. If this was all that was required, it would be an easy fix. It is much more a matter of accounting needing to reach a new plane of comprehension where digital comes to be understood as enabling new decision capabilities from which growth can occur and, in the process, spurring more growth from the data emanating from actions taken. Technological change, accounting information, and decision-making must all interface such that organizational performance evidences the absence of distance between data capture, analysis, and action.

Professional accountants have always been taught that their role is largely tied to providing relevant information for decision-making whether for internal organizational deployment or for external parties to make investment, compliance, and governance decisions. But the realization that is now essential on the part of finance leaders is that not understanding the power being unleashed by digital technologies is a dereliction of their role as to what they must bring to assurance work and to the management table.

NOTES

1. Goodfellow, J. 2020. Martin Sorrell: Coronavirus will trigger 'Darwinian Cull' of ad industry. Campaign (April 29). https://www.campaignlive .co.uk/article/martin-sorrell-coronavirus-will-trigger-darwinian-cull-ad-industry/1681758

2. Narayandas, D., Hebbar, V., and Li, L. 2020. Lessons from Chinese Companies' response to Covid-19. *Harvard Business Review* (June 5). https://hbr.org/ 2020/06/lessons-from-chinese-companies-response-to-covid-19

3. Dahl, et al. 2020. *Lessons from Asian Banks on their coronavirus response.* McKinsey & Company (March 25). https://www.mckinsey.com/industries/ financial-services/our-insights/lessons-from-asian-banks-on-their-coronavirus-response#

4. Ping An. 2020. Ping An Bank named Asia's best digital bank by Euromoney, a first for Chinese Bank. *Cision: PR Newswire* (July 24). https:// www.prnewswire.com/news-releases/ping-an-bank-named-asias-best-digital-bank-by-euromoney-a-first-for-chinese-bank-301099350.html

5. Bhimani, A. 2017. *Financial Management for Technology Start-Ups: A Handbook for Growth.* Kogan Page.

6. Morgan, B. 2019. *100 Stats on Digital Transformation and Customer Experience.* Forbes (December 16). https://www.forbes.com/sites/blakemorgan/2019/ 12/16/100-stats-on-digital-transformation-andcustomer-/

7. *2019 CFO Survey Report. All systems go: CFOs lead the way to a digital world.* 2019. Grant Thornton. https://www.grantthornton.ae/globalassets/2019-cfo-survey-report.pdf

8. Chan, J. 2020. *The widening skill gap in accountancy. Accountancy Age* (January 13).https://www.accountancyage.com/2020/01/13/the-widening-skill-gap-in-accountancy/

9. *Big Data; Big Opportunities.* 2020. Wolters Kluwer. https://xcmsolutions .com/resources/white-paper/big-data;-big-opportunities

10. Webb, C. 2020. The digital accountant: Digital skills in a transformed world. ACCA Global. https://www.accaglobal.com/in/en/professional-insights/technology/The_Digital_Accountant.html

11. Matthews, D. 2020. New ICAEW President backs 'warrior accountant' call. ICAEW. https://www.icaew.com/insights/viewpoints-on-the-news/2020/june-2020/new-icaew-president-backs-warrior-accountant-call

12. Izza, M. 2020. Risks and assurance of new tech: the next phase. ICAEW. https://www.icaew.com/insights/viewpoints-on-the-news/2020/aug-2020/risks-and-assurance-of-new-tech-the-next-phase

13. Thomas, M. 2020. *UK CEOs target digital success with investment in people and skills.* PwC. https://www.pwc.co.uk/ceo-survey/insights/marissa-thomas-case-study.html

14. Hood, T. 2020. *7 Skills Every Accountant Needs in the Age of Automation.* https:// blogs.oracle.com/modernfinance/7-skills-every-accountant-needs-in-the-age-of-automation

15. Sorbe, et al. 2019. *Digital Dividend: Policies to Harness the Productivity Potential of Digital Tchnologies.* OECDilibrary (February 12). https://www .oecd-ilibrary.org/economics/digital-dividend-policies-to-harness-the-productivity-potential-of-digital-technologies_273176bc-en

16. Nielsen, S. 2020. *Management Accounting and the Idea of Machine Learning.* Economics Working Papers 2020-09, Department of Economics and Business Economics, Aarhus University.

17. Kruskopf, et al. 2020. Digital accounting and the human factor: Theory and practice. *ACRN Journal of Finance and Risk Perspectives* 9: 78–89. http:// www.acrn-journals.eu/resources/SI08_2019a.pdf

18. Dharaiya, D. 2020. Does artificial intelligence help fight financial fraud? *readwrite* (January 16). https://readwrite.com/2020/01/16/does-artificial-intelligence-help-fight-financial-fraud/

19. *How an AI application can help auditors detect fraud.* 2020. https://www.ey. com/en_gl/better-begins-with-you/how-an-ai-application-can-help-auditors-detect-fraud

20. *Anomaly detection at Accenture.* 2020. https://www.accenture.com/gb-en/case-studies/about/anomaly-detection

21. Purcell, B. 2020. Who is responsible for responsible AI? *ZDNet* (August 17). https://www.zdnet.com/article/who-is-responsible-for-responsible-ai/

22. Baquero, et al. 2020. *Derisking AI by design: How to build risk management into AI development.* McKinsey & Company (August 13). https://www.mckinsey.com/business-functions/mckinsey-analytics/our-insights/derisking-ai-by-design-how-to-build-risk-management-into-ai-development#

23. Bernard, J., Nicholson, M., and Golden, D. 2020. *Reshaping the cybersecurity landscape.* Deloitte (July 24). https://www2.deloitte.com/us/en/insights/industry/financial-services/cybersecurity-maturity-financial-institutions-cyber-risk.html

24. Gordon, L., and Loeb, M. 2012. The economics of information security investment. *ACM Transactions on Information and System Security* 5 (4): 438–457.

25. Taleb, N., and Yam, Y. 2020. The UK's coronavirus policy may sound scientific. It isn't. *The Guardian* (March 25). https://www.theguardian.com/commentisfree/2020/mar/25/uk-coronavirus-policy-scientific-dominic-cummings

26. European Commission. 2019. *Ethics Guidelines for Trustworthy AI.* https://ec.europa.eu/futurium/en/ai-alliance-consultation

27. Saltelli, A. 2020. Ethics of quantification or quantification of ethics? *Futures* 116. https://doi.org/10.1016/j.futures.2019.102509

28. Saltelli, A., and Fiore, M. 2020. From sociology of quantification to ethics of quantification. *Humanities and Social Sciences Communications* (August 19), https://www.nature.com/articles/s41599-020-00557-0

29. Melancon, B. 2020. *Robots on the Rise: Automation in the Accounting Profession.* CIO Review. https://psa.cioreview.com/cxoinsight/robots-on-the-rise-automation-in-the-accounting-profession-nid-27321-cid-159.html

Resources

ON DIGITAL TECHNOLOGIES AND BUSINESS MODELS

Andres, P., Fritz, T., Lattwein, C., and Staglich, J. (2019). *Digital Transformation of the Finance Function: How the Finance Function Remains Relevant in the New World of Big Data and Analytics*. Oliver Wyman.

Beatty, C., and Crepaldi, N. (2020). *The Global Agenda: Asia-Pacific*. MIT Technology Review Insights.

Bizarro, A. P., Garcia, A., and Moore, Z. (2019). *Blockchain Explained and Implications for Accountancy*. ISACA.

CGMA. (2019). *CGMA Competency Framework*. www.cgma.org/resources/tools/cgma-competency-framework.html

Chandra, K., Plaschke, F., and Seth, I. (2018). *Memo to the CFO: Get in Front of Digital Finance – or Get Left Back*. McKinsey & Company.

Dahl, J., Sengupta, J., and Ng, E. (2020). *Future of Asia Banking: How Asia Is Reinventing Banking for the Digital Age*. McKinsey & Company.

Farrar, M. (2019). *Re-Inventing Finance for a Digital World. The Future of Finance*. CGMA. www.cgma.org/content/dam/cgma/resources/reports/downloadabledocuments/future-whitepaper-executive-summary.pdf

Govindarajan, V., Rajgopal, S., and Srivastava, A. (2018). Why financial statements don't work for digital companies. *Harvard Business Review*. hbr.org/2018/02/why-financial-statements-dont-work-for-digital-companies

Hewlin, T., and Snyder, S. (2019). *Goliath's Revenge: How Established Companies Turn the Tables on Digital Disruptors*. Wiley.

Iansiti, M., and Lakhani, R. K. (2020). *Competing in the Age of AI: Strategy and Leadership When Algorithms and Networks Run the World*. Harvard Business Review Press.

Klimas, T. (2020). DNA of the CFO: Is the future of finance new technology or new people? EY. www.ey.com/en_us/consulting/is-the-future-of-finance-new-technology-or-new-people

Loucks, J., Macaulay, J., Noronha, M., and Wade, M. (2016). *Digital Vortex: How Today's Market Leaders Can Beat Disruptive Competitors at Their Own Game*. Dbt Center Press.

Lyons, T., and Courcelas, L. (2020). *Convergence of Blockchain, Ai and Iot*. EU Blockchain Obervatory and Forum.

Manyika, J., and Woetzel, J. (2020). *No Ordinary Disruption: The Four Global Forces Breaking All the Trends*. McKinsey Global Institute.

McCann, D., Hall, M., and Warin, R. (2018). *Controlled by Calculations? Power and Accountability in the Digital Economy*. New Economics Foundation.

McGhee, M., and Grant, S. (2019). *Audit and Technology*. ACCA.

Morganti, T., and Schloemer, J. (2020). *Crunch Time. Reporting in a Digital World for Insurance Leaders*. Deloitte.

Narisetti, R. (2020). *The Next Normal: The Recovery Will Be Digital*. McKinsey & Company.

OECD. (2018). *Financial Markets, Insurance, and Private Pensions: Digitalisation and Finance*. www.oecd.org/competition/financial-markets-insurance-and-pensions-2018.htm

One Stream. (2019). *Finance Unleashed: Enabling Modern Finance with CPM 2.0 Platforms*. info.onestreamsoftware.com/white-paper-finance-unleashed-enabling-modern-finance-with-cpm-2.0-platforms

Pawczuk, L., Massey, R., and Holdowsky, J. (2019). *Deloitte's 2019 Global Blockchain Survey, Blockchain Gets Down to Business*. Deloitte Insights.

Ruckeshauser, N. (2017). *Do We Really Want Blockchain-Based Accounting? Decentralised Consensus as Enabler of Management Override of Internet Controls*. Institute of Computer Science and Social Studies, Department of Telematics, Freiburg, Germany.

Salijeni, G., Samsonova-Taddei, A., and Turley, S. (2019) Big Data and Changes in Audit Technology: Contemplating a Research Agenda. *Accounting and Business Research*, 49(1): pp. 95–119.

Sandra, G. (2019). Process Challenges of Big Data – A Comprehensive Study. *International Journal of Science and Research*, 8(11).

Westerman, G., Bonnet, D., and McAfee, A. (2014). *Leading Digital: Turning Technology into Business Transformation*. Harvard Business Review Press.

ON DIGITALIZATION AND COST MANAGEMENT

Curzi, Y., Fabbri, T., Scapolan, C.A., and Boscolo S. (2019). Performance appraisal and innovative behavior in the digital era. *Frontiers in Psychology*. www.frontiersin.org/articles/10.3389/fpsyg.2019.01659/full

Kiron, D., and Spindel, B. (2019). Redefining performance management at DBS Bank. *MIT Sloan Management Review*, Case Study.

Schrage, M., Kiron, D., Hancock, B. and Breschi, R. (2019). Performance management's digital shift. *MIT Sloan Management Review*, Research Report.

ON AI, RISK, AND AUDIT

Agrawal, A., Gans, J., and Goldfarb, A. (2018). *Prediction Machines: The Simple Economics of Artificial Intelligence*. Harvard Business Review Press.

Anant, V., Banerjee, S., Boehm, J., and Li, K. (2020). *A Dual Cybersecurity Mindset for the Next Normal*. McKinsey & Company.

Appelbaum, D., Kogan, A., and Vasarhelyi, A. M. (2017). Big Data and Analytics in the Modern Audit Engagement: Research Needs. *Auditing: A Journal of Practice & Theory*. 36(4): pp. 1–27.

Bizarro, A. P., Garcia, A., and Moore, Z. (2019). *Blockchain Explained and Implications for Accountancy*. ISACA.

Dutta, D. (2020). The Definitive Guide to Blockchain for Accounting and Business: Understanding the Revolutionary Technology. Emerald.

Fuller, H. S., and Markelevich, A. (2019). Should accountants care about blockchain? *The Journal of Corporate Accounting and Finance*. online library.wiley.com/doi/abs/10.1002/jcaf.22424.

ICAEW. (2018). *Blockchain and the future of accountancy*. www.icaew.com/technical/technology/blockchain/blockchain-articles/blockchain-and-the-accounting-perspective

Smith, S. (2018). Digitization and financial reporting – How technology innovation may drive the shift towards continuous accounting. *Accounting and Finance Research*. 7(3).

Tiberius, V., and Hirth, S. (2019). Impacts of digitization on auditing: A Delphi study for Germany. *Journal of International Accounting, Auditing and Taxation*. 37(C). ideas.repec.org/a/eee/jiaata/v37y2019ics1061951819300084.html

ON TRAINING AND ETHICS

Baquero, A. J., Burkhardt, R., Govindarajan, A., and Wallac, T. (2020). *Derisking AI by Design: How to Build Risk Management into AI Development*. McKinsey Analytics.

Briggs, B., Buchholz, S., and Sharma, S. (2020). *Tech Trends*. Deloitte Insights. www2.deloitte.com/content/dam/Deloitte/pt/Documents/tech-trends/TechTrends2020.pdf

Campolo, A., Sanfilippo, M., Whittaker, M., and Crawford, K. (2017). *AI Now 2017 Report*. ainowinstitute.org/announcements/ai-now-2017-report.html

Fidler, D. (2016). *Future Skills*. Act Foundation.

Grant Thornton. (2019). *CFO Survey Report*. All Systems Go: *CFOs Lead the Way to a Digital World*. CFO Survey Report.

McCann, D., Hall, M., and Warin, R. (2018). *Controlled by Calculations? Power and Accountability in the Digital Economy*. New Economics Foundation.

UNCTAD *Value Creation and Capture: Implications for Developing Countries*. (2019). Digital Economy Report 2019. unctad.org/webflyer/digital-economy-report-2019

Index